Things
I Wish
I'd Known
Before
My Child
Became
a Teenager

Things I Wish I'd Known Before My Child Became a Teenager

Gary Chapman

NORTHFIELD PUBLISHING

CHICAGO

Edited by Elizabeth Cody Newenhuyse
Interior design: Ragont Design
Cover design: Kelsey Fehlberg
Author photo: P.S. Photography

Library of Congress Cataloging-in-Publication Data

Names: Chapman, Gary D., 1938- author.
Title: Things I wish I'd known before my child became a teenager / Gary
    Chapman.
Description: Chicago : Northfield Publishing, 2021. | Includes
    bibliographical references. | Summary: "The teenage years are hard for
    everyone. Physical changes in your child create a lot of ups and downs.
    Yet as a parent, you don't have to feel helpless. Let Gary Chapman help
    you guide your child through this challenging yet rewarding new stage of
    life"-- Provided by publisher.
Identifiers: LCCN 2021022374 | ISBN 9780802425072 (paperback) | ISBN
    9780802476739 (ebook)
Subjects: LCSH: Parent and teenager. | Parenting. | Teenagers. | BISAC:
    FAMILY & RELATIONSHIPS / Parenting / General
Classification: LCC HQ799.15 .C47 2021 | DDC 306.874--dc23
LC record available at https://lccn.loc.gov/2021022374

All websites and phone numbers listed herein are accurate at the time of publication but may change in the future or cease to exist. The listing of website references and resources does not imply publisher endorsement of the site's entire contents. Groups and organizations are listed for informational purposes, and listing does not imply publisher endorsement of their activities.

We hope you enjoy this book from Northfield Publishing. Our goal is to provide high-quality, thought-provoking books and products that connect truth to your real needs and challenges. For more information on other books and products that will help you with all your important relationships, go to northfieldpublishing.com or write to:

Northfield Publishing
820 N. LaSalle Boulevard
Chicago, IL 60610

1 3 5 7 9 10 8 6 4 2

Printed in the United States of America

Contents

Dedication

To my wife, Karolyn Chapman, who walked with me on the journey of rearing our two teenagers.

Introduction

No one told me that something happens in the brains of children when they become teenagers. I was not prepared for this reality. I had assumed that the seven years between thirteen and twenty would simply be a continuation of the slow, predictable pattern of growth observed in childhood. I was not ready for the explosions, the emotional mood swings, and the unpredictable behavior.

If you read my earlier book *Things I Wish I'd Known Before We Became Parents*, you will know that Karolyn and I have two children, four years apart in age. They were very different in the way they processed life as teenagers, which leads me to a fundamental observation. There is no one pattern that can be applied to all teenagers. However, there are common physical, emotional, and neurological changes taking place in the teenage years.

Everyone agrees that the teenage years are extremely important in transitioning from childhood to young adulthood. The decisions that are made during these formative years will greatly impact the individual for the rest of their life. We are all keenly aware that some teens choose destructive lifestyles that impair their cognitive and physical abilities, which sometimes leads to an early death. This is one of the great tragedies of modern Western culture.

I also think most people agree that parents play a key role in the life of their teenagers. Absentee or abusive parents have a profound negative influence on the teen's behavior. At the same time, parents who are deeply committed to each other and are sincerely trying to give guidance to their teenager have a profound positive influence on the teen.

Please don't hear me saying that if parents do their job right, the teen will automatically become a responsible adult. We all know teens who grew up in loving, supportive families who made poor decisions that resulted in devastating consequences. Many of these parents have sat in my counseling office through the years. Their most common response is, "What did we do wrong?" Their assumption is that if they had done parenting well, their teen would not have made such decisions. The reality is that teens are human, and humans are free to make decisions, some of which result in much pain. Accepting this reality does not erase the pain, but does lead us to rise above our present discouragement and ask, "What can we do to help now?" Assuming the teen is alive, there is always the hope of redeeming the future.

Acknowledging the reality of human freedom does not diminish the fact that parents do play a major role in helping the teen process life in a positive manner. My purpose in writing this book is to help parents better understand the dynamics of the teen years, and thus be more effective parents. These dynamics have not changed—although some of the specific behaviors or expressions have. I am fully aware that many of my readers will be single moms. If you have a teenager, son or daughter, and their father is not involved in their life, I would encourage you to look for trusted adults who can play a significant part in the life of your growing teen. It may be a close relative, someone in your church, or a friend. Fortunate is the young man or young woman who has wise adults to turn to.

In addition to our own experience of parenting, I will be drawing on the scores of couples who have sat in my counseling office over the last forty years and shared their frustrations and, sometimes, deep pain in the rearing of their own teenagers. It is worth pointing out that although some things in the lives of teens have changed tremendously over the last few decades, the basic questions, longings, and struggles have not. Teens still seek independence. They're trying to find their place in the world. They don't always make the best decisions. And they still need you, even though it may not always seem that way.

In the following pages I will share twelve things I wish I'd known before we became parents of teenagers. The ideal time to read this book is when your children are eleven or twelve. The more prepared you are, the more likely you are to have positive responses to the changes that will take place when your children become teenagers. If your children are already teenagers, I think you will have a felt need to read this book, and I hope you will find it helpful in navigating the sometimes-turbulent waters of the teenage years.

I am also grateful for the excellent contributions of Drew Hill, who has spent many years working with teenagers. He has contributed a paragraph at the end of each chapter, along with an annotated list of the best contemporary and timeless resources available that relate to the topic of the chapter. I think you will find these resources very helpful.

I Wish I'd Known . . .

That Teens Are Developing the Ability to Think Logically

One mother said, "Why does my teenage son question everything I say? It's like something happened in his brain. He's never been like this before. It's like his whole personality has changed."

This mother unknowingly answered her own question. "It's like something happened in his brain." She is right. The teenage brain is going through a remodeling process. Don't expect your teenager to continue to be a child. Adolescence is all about change. We know that their bodies are changing because we can observe they are getting taller. We know they are changing sexually because pubic hair is beginning to form. The young teenage girl will soon begin her menstrual cycle if she hasn't already, and the young man will soon begin shaving his face. However, we are not always aware that they are changing mentally because we can't observe the brain. Research indicates that adolescence is a period of radical neurological change. One of those changes is that they are developing the ability to think logically.

Notice I say "developing" the ability to think logically. It doesn't happen overnight. Adolescence is a passageway between childhood and adulthood. In the early stages of development, the teen may dip back into childhood behavior and accept everything you say as fact, and two days later they may question everything you say. Because the teenage brain is impressionable, that is, greatly influenced by their environment, the parental role becomes extremely important in the teenage years. This is not the time to check out, but a time to walk with them through this ongoing renovation of the brain while they develop logical thought.

Another significant change in the teenage brain has to do with the emotional center of the brain. The teenager's emotional highs are extremely high, and the emotional lows are extremely low. This is because the emotional control center of the brain is also undergoing renovation. Your teen may be exceedingly happy in the morning and deeply sad in the evening of the same day. It all depends on what they encounter during the day. Remember, the teenage brain is hugely affected by the teen's environment.

As parents, you are a part of the teen's environment. The way you respond to their emotional state and their intellectual questions will determine whether you are a positive or negative influence on their developing brain. All of these changes are to be expected in the adolescent years. I wish I had known all of this before our children became teenagers. In this chapter and in each of the following chapters, I want to share some of the things I learned from my own experience, and some of the insights I've gained from parents who have come to me for counseling through the years.

STAYING ENGAGED

My first suggestion is to stay engaged. All research indicates that if parents will stay positively engaged with their teenagers, they will have a greater influence than will his or her peers. In the early days with my busy schedule I tended to respond quickly and without thought to my teens. If they questioned something that I thought we all had believed for some time, my response was something like, "You know better than that." Not a positive response. I was putting a cap on their questioning minds. They would walk away, and I had missed an opportunity to help them develop rational and logical thinking. Stay engaged, but the engagement must be positive.

Positive engagement begins with listening to the questions your teen is asking. As parents we are all busy but few things are more important than when our teen is asking questions. If you happen to be involved with something that you cannot stop immediately, then say, "That's an excellent question. Ask me again in ten minutes when I finish what I am doing because I want to give my full attention to what you are asking." Teens will accept that slight delay because they understand that you are interested in their question.

Don't assume that the first question your teen asks is the real question they want to ask. If they say to you, "Why can't I go to the party?" they may well be asking, "Have you thought this through, or are you simply making an arbitrary decision?" They want to know the reasons that led you to this conclusion. They may not be satisfied with your reasons, but they want to know that this was a thoughtful decision. And for the record, "Because I said so" is not a thoughtful response.

Don't expect your teen to always agree with the reasons you give. Remember, they are looking at the world from their limited perspective. You are still the parent. You have a position of authority over the teenager. You are older, and hopefully wiser, than your teen. Don't allow your teen's behavior to cause you to make a decision that you will later regret. If you "give in" to the request of your teenager because you want to avoid hysterical behavior, you will set a precedent. The teen will reason that if they can simply be obnoxious enough, they will get their way. That is not a behavioral pattern that will serve them well in adulthood.

Effective listening means that you will give your teenager your undivided attention when they are asking questions. Turn off the TV. Put your work aside. Put down your phone. Look them in the eyes and communicate silently that they are the most important person in your life at this moment. Once they have asked the question, you verbally affirm their question. "Good question. What brought that to your mind?" In that sentence you have affirmed their freedom to ask questions and you have also asked for more insight as to what led them to ask the question. That is important in knowing how you should respond.

EXPLORING A REAL-LIFE ISSUE

For example, one of the areas that most parents are deeply concerned about is the whole issue of alcohol and drug use in the teenage years. Research is clear that most adult alcoholics and drug abusers started the practice of drinking alcohol when they were teenagers. We don't want our teenagers to walk that road. But how do we help our teenager come to the same conclusion when their peers are encouraging them to drink and/or smoke marijuana? "If I catch you drinking or smoking marijuana, you will lose all of your privileges for the next three years" is not likely to keep your teen off of drugs and alcohol. However, utilizing your own experience, research, and exposure to real-life experience may well help your teen to make a logical decision about drugs and alcohol. Perhaps you had a relative who was an alcoholic. Be honest with your teen.

By real-life experience, I mean exposing your teen to the realities of what happens to teenagers when they become involved in alcohol and drugs. One of the best things I did with my son was to take him with me one Saturday a month to visit the juvenile detention center to play Ping-Pong with the young men who were incarcerated. After playing, we would engage in conversation with some of the young men and they would tell my son their story. I didn't have to say a word. They were proclaiming loudly the consequences of drug and alcohol abuse. On the drive home I would say to my son, "It's really sad, isn't it? Some of those guys are your age. It's so sad that they have made such poor decisions so early in life." He would readily agree, and sometimes make his own comments such as, "I hope I won't let anyone talk me into doing that." I would sometimes show him a news item about a teenager who had been killed in a car accident while under the influence of drugs or alcohol. I would say, "Derek, you might like to read this article. It's very sad, but it shows you what happens to some of the young people who drive while under the influence of drugs and alcohol."

If you are a parent who abused alcohol and drugs and you are now in the process of dealing with your addiction, you might consider taking your teenage son to your Alcoholics Anonymous group and let him hear the stories of other men, and also let him see some of your own struggle. He need not repeat your addictive pattern. As a matter of fact, the more knowledge he has of the struggle it has been for you, the more likely he is to make a wise decision about his own use of alcohol.

One young adult said to me, "The reason I decided as a teen not to drink alcohol or try drugs was because my father was an alcoholic. When I was twelve years old, he had an accident while driving under the influence, and a young mother in the other car was killed. After that, he enrolled in AA and was able to stay sober the rest of his life. But he never was able to shake the memory that his drinking had caused two young children to grow up without their mother. He fought bouts of depression the rest of his life. I knew that was not a road I wanted to travel."

In summary, I am saying that you can expect your teenager to ask "why" questions about almost any topic. They may even come across as being very argumentative, but you do not have to mirror their behavior. You can take their question seriously and have thoughtful answers. And when you do, you are helping them develop rational and logical thought. You are cooperating in a positive way with the neurological changes that are taking place in the brain of your teenager.

GOING DEEPER

If you want to help your teenager develop an ability to make wise decisions and think logically, one step you can take is to become more informed on your child's changes during adolescence. The more you grow in understanding these developmental challenges, the more compassion you will experience toward your children. When you show empathy and a willingness to learn, you demonstrate for your teen a picture of real maturity.

Below are a few resources that could be helpful in allowing you to step into your child's shoes.

Brainstorm: The Power and Purpose of the Teenage Brain —by Daniel J. Siegel, MD

This book is a fascinating and accessible explanation of the changes occurring in the teenage brain, specifically related to novelty seeking, social engagement, increased emotional intensity, and creative exploration. While these changes bring risks and negative possibilities, Dr. Siegel helps his readers understand both the downsides and upsides of adolescence.

CPYU.org

The Center for Parent/Youth Understanding, run by Dr. Walt Mueller, helps parents understand and connect with their preteens and teenagers. CPYU offers regularly updated "Youth Culture News," podcasts, articles, seminars, and other resources on adolescent development and culture.

Driven to Distraction: Recognizing and Coping with Attention Deficit Disorder—by Edward M. Hallowell, MD, and John J. Ratey, MD

Your teenagers are being raised in a world full of distractions. Even if your child does not experience ADD or ADHD, this book offers practical help for anyone who has trouble focusing, which is still the case for many undiagnosed teenagers.

IAmSecond.com

Stories impact teenagers more than bullet points. This website offers a wealth of video testimonies from actors, athletes, musicians, business leaders, addicts, survivors, and average joes. Their honest confessions address difficult topics like addiction, identity, and injustice. You likely will have an easier time getting your child to watch a ten-minute video than making them read an essay on addictions.

Coming Clean: A Story of Faith—by Seth Haines

The reality is that many teenagers are already wrestling with powerful addictions and haunting regrets. This raw and powerful memoir tells an honest story of healing from a recovering alcoholic. No matter what you or your teenager's escape is—social media, drugs, shopping, people-pleasing, food, alcohol, sex, you fill in the blank—Seth Haines's story offers hope for wholeness and a path for coming clean.

Help My Unbelief: Why Doubt Is Not the Enemy of Faith —by Barnabas Piper

Part of learning to think logically is learning to wrestle with faith and doubt. Teens need a safe space to ask questions and grapple with unbelief. This book will help you guide your children through those difficult conversations through the personal story of writer and pastor Barnabas Piper, himself the son of pastor and author John Piper.

Doubtless: Because Faith Is Hard—by Shelby Abbott

Being publicly skeptical about anything has become a cultural badge of honor in this digital age. Shelby Abbott humbly addresses the next generation's doubts with empathy and understanding. *Doubtless* is a book you could confidently read alongside your teenager.

THINK ABOUT IT

1. Reflect on your own teenage years. How did your parents respond when you disagreed with them? Were their responses helpful or harmful?

2. In what ways would you like to be different from your parents in responding to your teenagers?

3. In what ways would you like to emulate your parents' pattern of responding to your developing the ability to think logically?

4. If you already have teenagers, how would you evaluate the way you have responded when your teenager questions your judgment?

5. When you have exerted parental authority, have you done so in a firm but kind manner, or have you responded with harshness and anger?

6. What would you like to change about your past method of responding to your teenager?

7. If your children are not yet teenagers, what have you learned from this chapter that you think will be helpful to you when they begin to exhibit evidence that their brain is going through renovation, and they are beginning to think more logically and ask more questions?

Chapter 2

I Wish I'd Known . . .

That Culture Greatly Influences Teens

I should have been more in tune with the power of culture to influence belief and behavior. I had earned both a bachelor's and master's degree in cultural anthropology before our children became teenagers. I had studied various cultures around the world. I understood that the reason people have different belief systems and behavioral patterns is largely determined by the culture in which they grew up. However, I had failed to make the transition of applying that reality to my own teenagers. I had failed to think seriously about how the culture in which they were growing up was vastly different from the culture in which I grew up. And the culture today's teens are growing up in is vastly different from the one my son and daughter grew up in.

The culture in which I lived my teenage years was very homogeneous. Most of the people who lived in my neighborhood had the same fundamental beliefs about life. They had similar jobs. Ours was a southern textile town, and almost everyone worked at the textile mill, which operated twenty-four hours a day. Almost everyone had a garden in their backyard, which took up most of their nonworking hours in planting, cultivating, picking, and canning their own produce. Not everyone went to church on Sundays, but most did.

As a teenager I went to school during the day, worked in the garden in the afternoon, and played basketball on Saturdays in the backyard of my cousin's house. We went to church on Sunday mornings and often had lunch at the home of my aunt and uncle with other relatives on Sunday afternoon. Most of the time we went back to church on Sunday night. The only contact I had with the outside world was listening to NBC radio two or three times a week in the evening along with my mom, dad, and sister. I know it is hard to believe, but there was no TV when I became a teenager. I remember when I was fifteen my cousin's father bought a television set. It was the only one in the entire neighborhood, and the screen was black and white. I was fascinated that I could actually see the faces of people talking who lived in other cities.

Contrast my world with the world in which my own teenagers grew up. They had seen color television since the day they were born. Of course, in their childhood years we limited the number of programs they could watch, and we chose the programs. As they grew older, we gave them options between four or five shows, all of which we deemed acceptable—thus giving them the freedom to make decisions within boundaries. When they became teenagers, TV was not a new phenomenon in their lives; it was simply a part of life. Through television they were exposed to a much broader world than the one in which I grew up. They had known of the twenty-year war in Vietnam and the civil rights movement. As teenagers, they were glad the war was over, but they were asking serious questions about what it had accomplished. Their "why?" questions were hard to answer. The sexual revolution of the 1960s was over, but in the late '70s, as teenagers, they were living with the results.

As parents today, your teenagers are living in a very different world from the world in which my teenagers grew up. The quality and quantity of what is on television has been greatly expanded. My children had only the major networks. Today with streaming there is endless content available at all hours of the day. Personal computers were unknown to my teenagers, but to yours they are second nature. They cannot conceive of living life without digital devices. Smartphones give them access to most of what they can get on computers, plus allowing them to send messages and photos through texts, tweets, Instagram, TikTok, and numerous other platforms. Their world is exponentially broader than the world of my teenagers. Daily exposure to violence and tragedy around the world, discussion of issues from racism to climate change to immigration, images of wildfires and floods, and differing views of what makes a good society daily bombard the contemporary teenager. Open and honest discussion of mental health issues is far more accepted than it was a generation or two ago. Entertainment, gaming, and other online communities connect young people from Sydney to Seoul to Seattle. School communities are more diverse. School shooting drills are part of a student's day. Yes, their culture is radically different from the world of previous generations, and teens are greatly influenced by their culture. That is one thing that has not changed.

In my teenage years, if my neighbors saw me doing something that they knew was inappropriate, they would report it to my parents, and I knew that they would. Today your neighbors likely do not even know your teenagers. So what can the contemporary parent do to help their teen navigate the world in which they live? Let me make the following suggestions.

TEAMING UP ON TECHNOLOGY

Make technology work for you. Never before has information been so accessible as today. By pushing a few buttons or saying, "Hey, Siri!" you and your teen can learn almost anything you want to know. Therefore, use this tremendous resource. When you are discussing any topic with your teenager, suggest that each of you go online and see what you can find out about the subject. In doing so, you are teaching your teen how to make the most of technology. Of course, you need to advise your teen that not everything you read online and especially on social media will necessarily be true. The internet is awash in misinformation—some of it intentional and destructive. You will be doing your young teen a favor if you teach him or her critical thinking and discernment—and model it yourself.

A second value of technology is connectivity. You and your teen can now stay connected in a way that was impossible before smartphones. You can look at each other while you talk and even know where they are located at any given time. (Be sure your teen knows you have this ability. If they seek to thwart this ability, take the phone away for a week. After all, you are the one paying the bill.) Encourage your teen to text you and keep you informed with what is going on, and you do the same. Teens often prefer texting over talking on the phone. (You may too. Take advantage of that and "converse" with your teen through text.)

At the same time, it is very easy for a teen to get addicted to the screen, and it is up to you, the parent, to stay aware of their usage. They may be on social media or playing video games. But when their free time is consumed with the screen, it establishes a pattern they will take to adulthood, which will be detrimental to their marriage and adult relationships. Thus, setting boundaries is extremely important. Here are three suggestions.

First, there are certain things we do not watch. Pornography has become a major problem for contemporary teenagers. Pornography is a distortion of human sexuality. It imprints sexually explicit scenes on the human brain that are extremely difficult to erase. It degrades women. It leads the teen to live in an unrealistic world. As a parent, you should have open conversations with your teen about the dangers of pornography. Let them know that you have placed a screening device on their smartphone and computer that will seek to keep them from being exposed to pornographic sites. Seek to communicate this information out of a spirit of love and concern for their well-being, not out of a sense of an authoritarian parent.

Second, set time boundaries. Every teen needs screen-free time. One of these would certainly be mealtime. When teens or parents are looking at screens during mealtime, they are missing a wonderful opportunity for personal interaction. This is one thing that we did right when our teens were at home. The evening meal was a time for conversation. The television was off. The radio was not playing, and we did not answer the phone. We would often extend our conversations around the table for thirty minutes or more after the meal was over. I remember once when our son brought some friends home for a weekend his freshman year in college, we had our normal table conversations. His friends questioned him, "Do you guys always talk like that?" They admitted that their families never had such conversations. As adults, both of our children have told us that our mealtime conversation was one of their favorite memories.

I would also encourage limitations on how much time the teen watches television, or searches the web, or plays video games. Encourage them by taking walks with them in which *neither* of you looks at a screen or answers the phone or a text unless you see it is from a family member. Play board games together or shoot baskets in the backyard. If they are interested in sports, encourage them to play. If they are interested in music, encourage them to take lessons. Life is much bigger than the screen and we must help our teenagers understand this reality.

In addition to time boundaries, I would also encourage you to create space barriers, certain places where screens are not allowed. In addition to mealtimes, I would strongly encourage you to let the bedroom be a screen-free space—no TV, no laptop, no phone. (The exception would be if your daughter or son is doing homework on their device.) This is a boundary your teen may resist at first, but they will come back later and thank you. Of course, as parents we must also learn this lesson of limiting our screen time.

Such an idea is countercultural in contemporary society, where we feel we must be "plugged in" 24/7. But this boundary creates a place for the teen to be unplugged, and provides a great time for reading books. We will discuss this later, but teens who have regular reading times do better academically than those who don't. Of course, it is easier if you establish this boundary when they are children, and simply extend the practice into the teen years. However, it is never too late to set healthy boundaries.

In using technology, participate with your teen as often as possible. This may be watching television together. Whether it is a sporting event, a documentary, a newscast, or a movie, watch it together and afterwards discuss what you watched, what you learned, what messages were communicated, how excited you are at a sports win, and how disappointed you are at a sports defeat. It is these discussions that help you influence your teen rather than simply allowing the culture to influence him/her. We cannot remove the teen from the culture, but we can help them interpret the culture.

If they play sports, go to their game and discuss it afterwards. If they love the symphony, go to the symphony and discuss what you heard. If you have an interest that you would like to see your teen develop, take them with you, whether it be running, birding, photography, or any other interest you have. They may or may not be as excited as you are, but at least it gives them an opportunity to see you doing something you enjoy, and provides time for your teen to bond with you.

Since culture has such a profound influence on teenagers, let me encourage you to do everything you can to make sure the teachers at your teen's school are committed to helping your teen understand the value of education, encouraging their interests, and helping them develop a strong study ethic. Of course, teens are influenced not only by teachers but also by their peers. I know that you cannot choose their friendships, but encourage them to identify with students who are serious about learning.

Yes, your teenager is growing up in a world that is vastly different from the culture in which you grew up. Culture is constantly changing—sometimes in quick spurts as we have seen in the last sixty years, other times at a snail's pace. But culture never remains the same. Your teenager will not only be influenced by culture, but hopefully they will also influence cultural change. Imprint upon their mind the objective of leaving the world a better place than they found it. Demonstrate this in your own lifestyle and your teenager will likely accomplish the goal.

GOING DEEPER

As you consider the powerful influence the culture has on your children, it can feel overwhelming. Raising kids today has unique complications and challenges that past generations did not have to face. Some of the most challenging issues for parents to navigate are technology, screens, and social media.

The word "media" comes from a Latin root meaning "something that comes between." You may feel like devices and screens have already come between you and your adolescent child. If you need more help understanding how to handle technology with your teenager, below are eleven recommended resources.

Axis.org—a website, podcast, weekly email, and smartphone app

Axis is a nonprofit organization that specializes in helping parents understand the teenage culture. They offer a massive online library of resources that parents can access through a paid subscription, as well as a podcast and a free weekly email called "The Culture Translator."

When to Get My Kid a Phone: Navigating the Tensions —a twenty-four-page mini-book by Drew Hill

Determining when to get your child a smartphone is a complicated yet critical decision. Award-winning author Drew Hill invites parents to view phone usage as a gradual training process, much like their child learning to drive a car.

The Tech-Wise Family: Everyday Steps for Putting Technology in Its Proper Place—by Andy Crouch

This book offers dozens of helpful tips for building healthy technology habits in the home. It asks provocative questions and provides practical answers.

12 Ways Your Phone Is Changing You—by Tony Reinke

This insightful book shows how our phones affect us more than we realize. Phones amplify our addiction to distraction. They change the way we treat one another, and they feed our craving for immediate approval and gratification. As we understand the dangers of how we are being formed, it leads us to practical disciplines that help preserve our technological health in the smartphone age.

Living into Focus: Choosing What Matters in an Age of Distractions—by Arthur Boers

Boers contrasts modern technology's isolating effects with communal focal practices such as shared meals, gardening, hospitality, walking, prayer, and reading aloud.

Screens and Teens: Connecting with Our Kids in a Wireless World—by Kathy Koch, PhD

Educator and learning expert Koch looks at "lies" teens learn from technology, shares practical advice, and offers self-assessments for parents.

Good Pictures, Bad Pictures: Porn-Proofing Today's Young Kids
—by Kristen A. Jenson and Debbie Fox

Many parents struggle to know when and how to talk with their children about the dangers of pornography. This read-aloud story is geared at elementary-aged kids. It provides a comfortable script for parents to begin this conversation before the teenage years.

Screen Kids—by Gary Chapman and Arlene Pellicane

In an era when toddlers love their iPads, it's never too early to start monitoring your child's (and your own) screen time. Dr. Chapman and Arlene Pellicane, the mom of two teens, share advice and encouragement.

Project Six 19: ProjectSix19.org/for-parents

This nonprofit organization provides videos, e-courses, books, and podcasts to help parents talk with their kids about sex, pornography, and sexuality.

ScreenagersMovie.com—SCREENAGERS: Growing Up in the Digital Age | SCREENAGERS: Next Chapter

These two documentaries show the impact of screen technology on the mental health of children and teenagers. They offer parents ideas on how to empower teens to overcome the emotional challenges associated with screen time.

Gen Z: The Culture, Beliefs, and Motivations Shaping the Next Generation—by **Barna Group**

If you want to better understand the culture of your teen's generation, this research-heavy resource will shed statistical insight on how teenagers view themselves, their spiritual lives, and the world around them.

THINK ABOUT IT

1. Share with your teen something of what the world was like when you were a teenager. They will likely find it fascinating.

2. Looking at your own teenage years, what regrets do you have?

3. What were the positive things about your teenage years of which you are proud?

4. In what ways did your parents positively or negatively affect you when you were a teenager?

5. What can you learn from their model?

6. Write a short paragraph on what you hope for your child between the ages of thirteen and eighteen. If you like what you have written, you might consider sharing it with your teenager.

Chapter 3

I Wish
I'd Known . . .
That Teens Need
to Feel Loved

At the age of thirteen, he ran away from home. Sitting in my office he said, "My parents don't love me. They love my brother, but they don't love me." I knew his parents and I knew they loved him, but obviously, there was a disconnect. In the counseling office, it is not unusual to find that one sibling feels loved by the parents and the other does not. Why this disparity? What many parents do not understand is that each of us has a primary love language. Years ago, I wrote a book entitled *The 5 Love Languages: The Secret to Love That Lasts*. It was written to married couples to help them keep emotional love alive after the "in love" euphoria fades.

By nature, a husband expresses love to his wife in the love

language that makes him feel loved. However, if that is not her love language, she will not feel loved. I discovered this concept in my counseling office, where I heard so many stories from couples who were missing each other emotionally. When a spouse does not feel loved, it is much more difficult to process the rest of the marriage relationship, such as solving conflicts and managing money. When they both feel secure in each other's love, life is beautiful. The book has sold millions of copies and has been translated and published in more than fifty languages around the world. Many couples have said to me, "That book saved our marriage."

This same concept can help parents effectively communicate love to their teenager. Most parents love their teenagers. However, many teens do not feel loved. Parents often assume that what makes one teen feel loved will make another teen feel loved. That is a false assumption. My research revealed that there are five basic "love languages," and that each teen has a primary love language. If parents do not express love in that language, the teen will not feel loved, even though the parent is speaking some of the other love languages. Let me briefly describe each of the five love languages.

Words of Affirmation—verbally affirming the teen. "You did a great job in the debate at school." "I really appreciate you helping me clean the garage." "I really like your smile; you are so handsome/ beautiful when you smile." "One of the things I appreciate about you is I know you will tell me the truth." Your comments may focus on how the teen looks, a personality trait, or some accomplishment.

Within each of the languages, there are various dialects. For example, words of encouragement are designed to instill courage to keep trying. Perhaps a teen is trying to learn to play a musical instrument. A parent might say, "I think you are making real progress.

You are definitely improving." Then there are words of praise, which identify something the teen did that you admire, such as: "I noticed the way you encouraged Adam after he missed that shot. I know he must have felt bad. All of us need encouragement when we are feeling bad."

In giving words of praise for the teen's accomplishments, always praise them for effort, not for perfection. I remember one teen who said to me, "I don't ever please my father. If I mow the grass, he complains that I did not get the grass under the bushes. If I make a double, he tells me I should have made a triple. If I make a B on my report card, he tells me I should have made an A."

I knew his father, and I knew what he was trying to do. He was trying to motivate his son to do his best. However, what the teen was hearing was condemnation. What a teen needs when he has mowed the lawn is "Thanks for mowing the grass. That is a real help to me." It is next week when he starts to mow that you call attention to the grass under the bushes. Because he feels loved and appreciated, he will take care of the grass under the bushes. Brag on the B and then next week say, "I wonder what you could do to bring that B to an A." Praise him for the double, and next Saturday show him how sometimes he can turn a double into a triple. Again, praise the teen for effort, not perfection.

Acts of Service—doing something for the teen that you know they would like for you to do. It might be fixing their favorite meal or dessert. Or, it could be helping them with their math homework assignment. When Connor's dad agreed to help him build the set for his high school drama production, he was speaking Connor's primary love language—acts of service. For these teens, "actions speak louder than words."

Sometimes we are doing things for the teen that they cannot do for themselves, such as ironing a shirt for your son who has a summer job interview, or changing a tire on your daughter's car. We can also speak this love language by teaching them to do things for themselves, such as teaching the son to iron a shirt and the daughter how to fix a flat tire. It might be easier to do it for them, but it might be more meaningful to teach them how to do it, especially if their love language is acts of service.

Receiving Gifts—giving the teen something you know they would appreciate. (This does not mean you give them everything they request.) You give them gifts that are in keeping with their stage of development, and that you think will be helpful. The gift need not be expensive. It may be a small candy bar you know is their favorite. Yes, it may include clothing and shoes, as long as it is something they like.

Please note that a gift is given as an expression of love, not in response to something the teen has done for you. "I'll buy you those new shoes if you will clean your room" is simply payment for services rendered, and not a gift at all. If receiving gifts is your teen's primary love language, present the gift deliberately. Don't say, "I got you a new shirt and put it in your closet." Rather, give it to them face-to-face saying, "because I love you." If the teen is a collector of baseball cards or anything else, keep that information on the front burner of your mind.

Some parents have asked, "Does this love language not foster an attitude of materialism in the mind of the teenager?" Only if you give the teen everything they request. It is true that teens who understand the love language concept may seek to manipulate you. "If you loved me, you would get me an Apple watch. You know receiving gifts is my love language." The parent's response? "I love you too much to give you an Apple watch now. That will come when you are older, but not now." For those whose primary love language is receiving gifts, it really is "the thought that counts." When you remember their favorite candy or hobby or other interests, and give them something you know they will like, it speaks loudly of your love.

Quality Time—giving the teen your undivided attention. Don't confuse quality time with simply being in the same room. You can watch a sports event on television with your teen, but it is not quality time unless before or after the game you talk with your teen about the game or whatever is on his/her mind. It might be taking your teen out to breakfast or lunch, just the two of you, and listening to their concerns. It is not responding to your phone when you are listening to your teen.

I remember a young teen who said to me that he did not feel loved by this father. When I asked why, he said, "We don't ever spend time talking." "I thought you told me that you and your father go to all of the Wake Forest football games together," I said. "We do, but he is into the game, not into me. I'm just another body sitting beside him. We don't talk on the way to the game, or at the game, or driving home after the game. Like I said, we don't ever talk." It was obvious to me that this teen's love language was quality time. He wanted his father's undivided attention. He did not feel loved by simply sitting beside his father at a football game.

Physical Touch—appropriate, affirming touches such as high fives, pats on the back, hugs, or back rubs. For these teens, physical touch is what makes them feel loved. Appropriate touches communicate "I see you. I know you. I love you." One observation I have made is that, in our overly sexualized culture and with the common reports of parental sexual abuse, some fathers tend to draw back from hugging their adolescent daughters. However, if the daughter's primary love language is physical touch and the father does not give her appropriate touches, she will begin to feel unloved. Sometimes, she will reach out to an older teenage boy who will give her physical touch, often inappropriately. She is less likely to fall into this trap if her father is expressing his love by giving her appropriate, affirming touches.

Please don't hear me saying that you only speak the teen's primary love language. The goal would be to give heavy doses of the teen's primary love language, and then sprinkle in the other four for extra emotional credit. Ideally, we want the teen to be able to receive and give love in all five languages. That is the teen who will most likely succeed in building healthy relationships as an adult. However, if you don't speak the teen's *primary* love language, they will not feel loved, even though you are speaking some of the other languages.

So why do parents often fail to speak the teen's love language? One reason is that the parent has never discovered the teen's primary love language. This problem can easily be solved. Ask yourself three questions: "How does my teen most often relate to other people?" If you hear your teen often giving affirming words to others, then his/her primary love language is most likely words of affirmation. If they are always doing things to help people, then acts of service may be their love language. Typically, we show love to others in the way we would like to receive love. "What does my teen complain about most often?" Do you hear your teen saying, "I can't ever please you!" If so, his love language is probably words of affirmation. If, when you return from the grocery store, your teen says, "You didn't buy me anything?" they are telling you that their love language is gifts. The teen's complaint reveals their love language. "What does my teen most often request?" My daughter as a teen would say, "Dad, can we take a walk after dinner?" She was asking for quality time. If you go on a business trip and your son says, "Be sure and bring me a surprise!" they are asking for a gift. "Would you give me a backrub?" reveals that their language is physical touch.

Your answer to those three questions will likely reveal clearly your teen's primary love language. You might also ask your teen to take the free love language profile located at 5lovelanguages.com. One mother said, "We asked our son to take the profile and were shocked to learn that his love language is quality time. We had always assumed it was words of affirmation, which we had given freely. It was amazing how our relationship improved when we started taking walks with him and giving him individual attention."

The second reason parents may find it hard to speak the teen's love language is that the parent never received that love language from their parents. One father said, "I know that my son's love language is physical touch, but my father never gave me hugs and I find it hard to hug my son. I see his mother hugging him and how much he likes it." The answer for this father is to take baby steps. Begin with a light bump on the shoulder as you walk by him, or a high five after some positive event. Then comes a pat on the shoulder. Such small steps lead to hugs.

The good news is that you can learn to speak any of the love languages as an adult, even if you did not receive them as a child. One father said, "My father never told me that he loved me. When my son came along, I vowed that I would say, 'I love you,' but I have to admit, it was hard. However, I am so glad I did, because now I know that words of affirmation is his love language."

A third reason that parents may find it difficult to speak the teen's love language is what we noted earlier: the teen is going through tremendous changes physically, emotionally, and intellectually. Even if you discovered and spoke their love language when they were younger, they may draw back from it when they become a teenager. A mother said, "I know that my daughter's love language is quality time. As a child she loved to play games with me and go shopping with me. Now she has no interest in those things." I am often asked, "Does their love language change when they become a teenager?" I don't think so, but you must learn new dialects of their love language. The ways you formerly expressed love seem childish to them now. Quality-time teens may prefer taking a hike together or going to a sports event and talking to you, rather than playing a game with you.

At ten years of age, his mom could hug him after his game with all his friends standing around, and he felt loved. Now, he pushes her away. He still needs physical touch, but it needs to be in private, not in front of his teammates.

When he/she was young, you could say, "You are so sweet. I love you so much." If words of affirmation is their love language, they still need affirming words, but they need to sound more adult, like "I really admire the way you took time to talk with Chloe; I could tell she was upset." So, as a parent, you don't need to learn a different language, just a different dialect.

As noted earlier, the teen's emotions are fluctuating greatly in response to what happens in life. A physical-touch teen may receive a hug from mom in the morning, but a hug in the afternoon may be rejected. Why? Something happened at school that impacted them emotionally. A good rule of thumb with hugs is: if the teen stands close to you, a hug will likely be received. But if they stand across the room, probably not. Try to read their moods and you will understand why your expressions of love may be accepted or rejected.

It is important for parents to understand that when you use their love language to express displeasure, the heart of the teen is greatly wounded. For example, if a teen's love language is words of affirmation, negative words spoken to them pierce like a dagger to the heart. When you lash out in anger at them with loud, harsh words, they feel rejected. They may lash back, or they may suffer in silence, but they will suffer.

If a teen's love language is physical touch and in anger you push, shove, or slap them, you have hurt them in the worst possible way. Nothing you could say or do would hurt them more deeply than physical abuse. If quality time is their love language and they feel ignored as they watch you spend all of your time working, golfing, or involved with younger siblings, they will feel detached from you. You may take them to a professional soccer match, but if your total attention is on the game, and your teen is treated like a stranger who happens to be sitting with you, they will walk away feeling emotionally empty.

If acts of service is the teen's love language and you promise to help them with a school project but later tell them you don't have time, you have just communicated that something else is more important than them.

No parents are perfect. All of us fail from time to time. Even if we know the teen's love language, we get busy with a thousand other responsibilities, and fail to meet their emotional need for love. We may even fall into the trap of expressing our frustration with the teen's behavior in a negative manner as described above. We don't have to be perfect to be good parents, but we do need to deal with our failures by apologizing to our teen when we fail.

Some parents think that their teen will lose respect for them if they apologize. The opposite is true—they will gain respect for you. They already know that what you did or said is not appropriate. They already feel the pain of your misbehavior. If you apologize, your teen will likely forgive you and the relationship can move forward in a positive manner.

I hope you are beginning to see how important it is for parents to discover and speak a teen's primary love language during these years of transition from childhood to adulthood. I like to picture inside every teenager an emotional "love tank." When the tank is full—that is, the teen feels deeply loved by the parents—the teen will grow up emotionally healthy. But when the love tank is empty, the teen will not feel loved. He/she will likely go looking for love, typically in all the wrong places. Few things are more important to the emotional health of a teenager than keeping the "love tank" full.

For more information on understanding and expressing your teen's love language, see *The 5 Love Languages of Teenagers*. Your teen might also want to read *A Teen's Guide to The 5 Love Languages*, written just for them. The teen might even discover that parents also have a love language.

A special word to those parents who are in a blended family: the emotional dynamics are very different between a teen and his or her stepparent. It is not enough to know the teen's primary love language. For example, perhaps you know that the teen's love language is physical touch. So, with every intention of communicating love, you reach out to them with a hug, and they push you back. Don't get discouraged. They simply have not yet developed an emotional bond with you. Yes, they need physical touch, but you must start with less intimate touches, like fist bumps, high fives, or shoulder bumps. It may take time before they are ready for a hug.

Understanding the intimacy level of the various dialects of a love language is important in a blended family. I would urge you to read *Building Love Together in Blended Families: The 5 Love Languages and Becoming Stepfamily Smart*, which I wrote with Ron Deal, who for over twenty-five years has helped stepparents relate to their stepchildren.

GOING DEEPER

Hidden underneath the confusing behaviors of your teenage children is a desperate longing to be loved. Teenagers are searching for answers to the more profound questions of life. They're trying to figure out who they are, where they belong, and if they matter, all while facing new realities of loneliness and isolation. It's a pivotal time of development. Even when it feels like they are pushing you away, they still want to be loved and pursued.

So how do you get to their hearts? The resources below provide a trusted map that points the way.

The 5 Love Languages of Teenagers: The Secret to Loving Teens Effectively—by Gary Chapman

This deeper dive into the five love languages helps explain more of teenagers' developmental changes and gives parents practical tools for communicating in their teen's love language. Parents and kids can both take a short test to determine their love language at 5lovelanguages.com.

A Teen's Guide to the 5 Love Languages—by Gary Chapman with Paige Haley Drygas

A teen-friendly guide to the love languages and how understanding them can help a teen's important relationships. This short, well-designed book will have great appeal for teens.

Alongside: Loving Teenagers with the Gospel—by Drew Hill

Alongside is a beautiful and practical companion for anyone who wants to learn how to better love the teenagers in their life. It's full of real-life stories of the gospel breaking through the distractions, darkness, loneliness, and pain that often accompany adolescence. It also offers super-practical tools to help you communicate that story well as you walk alongside your own children.

Heart Cries of Every Teen: Eight Core Desires That Demand Attention—by Jackie E. Perry, MS, LPCS

This book helps you understand the physical, social, emotional, cognitive, and psychological changes occurring during adolescence. These changes compel teenagers to look for ways to satisfy the new aches that arise. Perry helps parents recognize the true desires behind these behaviors and, in turn, learn to connect with their children instead of running the other way.

Growing With: Every Parent's Guide to Helping Teenagers and Young Adults Thrive in Their Faith, Family, and Future—by Kara Powell and Steve Argue

Many parents fear that the transition to adolescence means that the new teenager doesn't want or need a mom or dad anymore. But growing up doesn't have to mean growing apart. This research-rich book helps parents work toward solutions and dive into tough discussions about such topics as dating, career, and finances.

The Back Door to Your Teen's Heart: Learning What They Need and Helping Them Find It—by Melissa Trevathan and Sissy Goff

Written by seasoned counselors who have spent decades working with teenagers and families, this book communicates a deep understanding of what teenagers experience. With honest stories and real-life examples, Trevathan and Goff offer great encouragement and hope for parents who feel at the end of their ropes.

THINK ABOUT IT

1. Do you know your teen's primary love language? Do you know your own love language?

2. What steps suggested in this chapter could you take to clarify your teen's love language?

3. Try asking this question to your teen: "On a scale of 0–10, how much love do you feel coming from me?" Then, if they say anything less than 10, you might ask: "What could I do to bring it up?" Their answer will likely give you another clue as to their primary love language.

4. You might ask your spouse if he/she would be willing to ask your teen the same question. If both of you do so, your teen is probably going to ask: "What's going on? Why are you both asking me this question?" You can honestly say, "We are trying to learn how to be better parents. We love you, but we want to make sure you feel loved."

5. Would you be willing to ask your teen to take the free online profile for teenagers? Would you also be willing to take the free quiz for couples? Both are located at 5lovelanguages.com.

6. Is there something for which you need to apologize to your teen? If so, why not do it today?

Chapter 4

I Wish I'd Known . . .

That Teens Are Moving Toward Independence

By the time a teenager gets to be eighteen years of age, he or she needs to have developed some level of independence. At the age of eighteen they are typically finishing high school and moving toward college, the military, or getting a job (we hope). As parents, we know that we do not want our children living at home at the age of thirty with no job, no education, and no ambition. We anticipate that, when they get to be adults, they will be able to support themselves financially, make wise decisions, and have a positive impact on society. We want them to be "givers," not "takers." We want them to enrich the world, and not be dependent upon parents or others for their survival.

If our children are to become responsible adults, then the process must begin in the teenage years. Deep within the teenage psyche is the desire for independence. Something happens in the teenage brain that triggers the thought, "My parents have done things for me all of my life. They have made all of my decisions. Now it's time for me to make some of my own decisions. I can take care of myself. I am not a child anymore." I wish I'd known my role as a parent was to encourage this spirit of independence, rather than trying to squelch it. I wish I'd known that cooperating with this natural desire for independence is far better than trying to deter it or ignore it. I wish I'd known that the urge for independence is a good thing, not a bad thing, and that as a parent I needed to cooperate with and guide the process. Your son or daughter is starting to establish their own identity, discovering themselves—apart from you. You can help them through this journey.

THEIR OWN SPACE

The desire for independence will express itself in various aspects of life. One of the first places where the desire for independence emerges is the *desire for personal space*. Perhaps they have been living with a younger sibling and they will request their own bedroom. They may even say, "Can I move into the attic or the basement?" If you are able and choose to provide such personal space, they will decorate their room in a way that you cannot imagine. It is their way of convincing themselves, and you, that they are growing up. They are unique. They have likes and dislikes. They are a part of, and yet separate from, the family.

In social settings, this same desire for independence will lead them to desire to sit with their friends, rather than their family. Whether it is at sporting events, theaters, or church, they want to be seen as an individual, not simply as a part of the family. If they need or desire new clothes, they would prefer to buy them without you. However, if as a concerned parent you decide that since you are paying for the clothes you want to have the final word on what they buy, they will then request that you go shopping at a time when their friends will not be there. (Or just order online.) They do not wish to be seen with you, for that says in their mind that they are a child, and not a teenager.

In relating to extended family you may also find the teen demonstrating this move toward independence. So, you mention to your teenage son that Grandmother's birthday is next week and "we will be going to her birthday party next Saturday." Your teen may well say, "I don't want to go." As a parent, you are shocked because your family has gone to Grandma's birthday party since the children were young. Before you lash out in anger with, "You are going with us. She is your grandmother and we are going to celebrate her birthday," why not ask your son why he does not want to go? In so doing, you are treating him as a teen who is developing independence. If he says, "It's boring down there. All we do is sit around and talk. I want to have fun with my friends on Saturday," your response might be, "I can understand that. If I were your age, I probably would feel the same way. However, this is one time when we have to put family first." You have acknowledged that his feelings are valid, and you have not accused him of being disloyal to his grandmother. You are the parent and you are the one to make the final decision, but you can do so in such a way as to affirm his desire for independence.

All of these desires to be differentiated from you can be hard for the parent to process. A parent may see these actions as a lack of gratitude for what the parent has done for the teenager. "Why would they want to distance themselves from us when we are their family?" is a question that many parents have asked. The answer is simple: they are moving toward independence.

Teens may also *desire emotional space.* They may not be as talkative as they were when they were children. They may tend to keep their thoughts and feelings to themselves. When you ask them, "What's going on?" their answer may well be, "Nothing." As a child they freely shared their emotions, but as a teen they may be reluctant to say, "I'm afraid that I might not pass algebra." Or, "I'm sad because my friend at school doesn't want to be my friend anymore." The teen wants to appear strong and self-sufficient. Young men often feel reluctant to share their emotions because they think to do so is a sign of weakness. They may pull back from your expressions of love. This can be painful for parents who do not understand what is going on in the mind and emotions of the teenager.

For the teenager, their emotions are like a roller coaster, fluctuating throughout the day. They may be on a high one moment, and an hour later on a low, depending on the circumstances they have encountered throughout the day. They often do not want their parents to know how they are feeling, because they don't want the parent to jump in and try to do something about the situation that stimulated the emotions. One teen said, "I didn't tell my parents that the teacher gave me a 'D' on my paper because I told her that my dad helped me write it. I knew they would go talk with the teacher and that would get me into more trouble."

The teen's move toward independence often involves withdrawing emotionally. If parents understand this reality, they will not interpret this as rejection.

There are numerous ways in which a teen expresses their move toward independence. They will likely prefer a music style different from your own. Their choice will be greatly impacted by the popular music style of the culture at the time. To criticize the teen's music is to criticize the teen. It's their choice and you are condemning their choice. Far better for you to read the lyrics to the songs and make positive comments where you can. I say read the lyrics because you may not be able to understand the lyrics as they are sung by your child's favorite musician.

This is one area where I feel like I did it right. I remember when my son got into Buddy Holly and later Bruce Springsteen. (I know that some of you are not old enough to remember Buddy Holly, a '50s rocker.) I read the lyrics of the songs and looked for things about which I could be positive and communicated them to my son. On one occasion I said to him, "Derek, I'm going to speak in Fort Worth, Texas. How would you like to go with me? And when I finish speaking, you and I can drive out to Lubbock and discover Buddy Holly's hometown." He replied, "Ohhhhh! I would love to do that!" (I had no idea how far it was from Fort Worth to Lubbock. It's a long ride.)

We spent a whole day following the guidelines given to us by the Chamber of Commerce. We went to the house where he was born, the schools that Buddy attended, the church where he was married and where they had his funeral, the radio station that played his first record, the Cotton Club where he played locally, and the cemetery where he is buried. As we drove back from Lubbock to Fort Worth we talked about all that we had seen and heard, and wondered what would have happened if Buddy Holly had not been killed in the plane crash that took his life decades ago. To be totally honest, I was not interested in Buddy Holly (he was already dead) but I was interested in my son and I wanted him to know that I appreciated his taste in music.

Later, we made a similar trip to Bruce Springsteen's home in New Jersey. Then, when my son went to college and took a music appreciation course, he joined the symphony. That's when I learned what an oboe is. What I'm saying is that when we express appreciation for our teenager's choices and look for the good in those choices, we are affirming their independence and their ability to make wise decisions.

You may also discover that your teenager begins to speak a different language. They will use words that you have never heard. Again, it is the culture's way of helping teenagers express their independence. They have code words that are meaningful to teenagers, but not to adults. They will want to wear clothes that you find hard to imagine. Their hairstyle or color may at times shock you, along with various tattoos and piercings. I remember when our son came home from his first semester of college with orange hair, and later that year with no hair. Yes, he looked very different from me, but he was in the process of expressing his independence and I came to see that for what it was.

For the parent who is uninformed or fails to focus on the natural move toward independence in the teenage years, these things may be disturbing. Their tendency will be to condemn or at least question the teenager. In so doing, they create an emotional barrier between the two of them. However, when we affirm our teenager's move toward independence, we are preparing them for adulthood.

INDEPENDENCE—WITH RESPONSIBILITY

With developing independence comes developing responsibility. When your teenager becomes an adult and moves away from home, he or she will be free to make all of their decisions. However, they need to learn the reality that with every decision there are consequences—negative or positive, depending on the wisdom of the decision. If they have never learned to be responsible for the decisions they make and thus accept the consequences, they will likely have marital difficulties. Who wants to live with an irresponsible spouse, one who wants independence without responsibility?

This attitude of responsibility must be learned in the teenage years along with the move to independence. There are many venues from which to teach responsibility. For example, along with the opportunity to have their own personal space in the attic or basement or perhaps an extra bedroom, the teen must accept the responsibility for dusting all the decorations they choose to put in their room and they must be responsible for vacuuming or sweeping the floor once a week. If they fail in their responsibilities, then there must be appropriate consequences.

One big test of responsibility arrives when the teen becomes old enough to drive a car. This is a rite of passage for teenagers. Most anticipate the day when they will be able to drive. I have long urged parents to impress on their teen the reality that with the privilege of driving the car comes the responsibility of putting gas in the car in a timely fashion, or running the vehicle through the carwash when needed. Most teens will gladly respond to that request if it accompanies the freedom to drive the family car, or a car that you may have helped them purchase. If they fail at their responsibility, they lose the privilege of driving the car for two days, the second offense four days, and the third offense one week. I can almost guarantee they will not lose the privilege of driving the car more than once or twice. More importantly, they are learning that with independence comes responsibility.

With the freedom to drive a car also comes the obligation to abide by local traffic laws. If the teen violates these laws, whether ticketed by the police or observed by the parent, again they should lose driving privileges for a significant amount of time.

If you provide a phone at whatever age you feel appropriate, with that decision should come the teen's commitment to use their device responsibly. The parent should have full access to their teen's phone. If they use the phone to bully others, send inappropriate photos or texts, view pornography, or anything else you consider detrimental to their development, they lose the phone for a stipulated period of time. Again, independence and responsibility must go together.

Pet care is another area where teens can practice responsibility. My grandson at the age of thirteen begged his mom and dad for a dog. My daughter, his mother, was not into dogs so she resisted. However, after due time, she conceded with one stipulation: "If we get you a dog, you will be responsible for feeding, watering, and washing the dog." He agreed. So, Kona came to live at their house, and my grandson learned that with freedom to have a dog comes the responsibility to take care of the dog. Kona was an older dog and already well trained, so he did not have the responsibility of training a dog. A few years later when Kona died, I asked him if he was going to get another dog. He responded, "No, Papa, I've done that." I will be interested to see if he gets a dog when he becomes an adult.

Every member of the family should have age-appropriate

responsibilities. There is much to be done in a household to simply maintain the normal flow of life. Someone must cook meals, wash dishes, vacuum the floors, get the white spots off the mirror, clean the toilet, walk the dog, and so forth. If children grow up having responsibilities in the home, they will likely be more willing to accept your efforts in teaching greater responsibilities in the teenage years.

We need to teach responsibilities *and* teach the required skills. I suggest that parents and teenagers compile a list of all the things they would like for their teen to be able to do by the time they turn eighteen. These would include the household responsibilities mentioned above. But they would also include how to operate a lawn mower, how to change the dust bag in the vacuum, how to wash and dry laundry, how to buy groceries, and how to cook a meal. As a parent, you may be surprised at some of the things your teenager would like to learn how to do. If your family is involved in boating, skiing, fishing, hunting, or other recreational activities, the teen needs to learn all of the skills and safety rules associated with those activities. If the parents and the teen have a clear vision of the skills they would like for the teen to know by the age of eighteen, and you consistently teach the skills and hold the teenager responsible, you will likely live to see your teenager become a responsible adult.

Careful money management is a must for all adults, and it should start young. But teens can't manage money if they have no money. There are two options to resolving this dilemma. One is the teen may acquire a part-time job. This is possible if they are not involved in playing sports or other extracurricular school activities. However, if they are so involved, the parents may choose to give them a weekly or monthly allowance and clearly define what the teenager is to buy out of that money. At some stage I suggest that you open a checking account for your teenager so that they learn how to balance a monthly bank statement. Encourage them to save a certain percentage of the money they receive and to give away a certain percentage of the money they receive. Saving and giving will both enrich the life of a teenager. Responsible money management is a skill that will be greatly needed when they become an adult.

One of the tragedies of our day is that many teenagers grow up in a home where they have no responsibilities. The parents take care of all the household responsibilities. The parents give them all the school supplies and everything else they need in life, but never teach them responsibility. These teens enter adulthood greatly handicapped.

Also, what general skills will your teen need to prepare him or her to enter today's workforce? Some skills will relate to technology and to being trained for future employment, regardless of the market sector. In addition, every teen needs "soft" but essential skills such as emotional intelligence and the ability to communicate effectively. These are crucial in their transition to adulthood.

I recently had dinner with a group of professional football players. The conversation turned to what they would do when they were no longer able to play football. One player said, "The problem is that we don't know how to do anything except play football. We have been playing since we were kids, and football is all we know." Other players chimed in in agreement. Then another player said, "I'm teaching my son how to operate a lawn mower." Another one said, "Well, my son has a friend whose father is a cabinetmaker and has a wood shop in his garage. So, my son and his friend are learning how to make furniture." I was impressed to see that these players were concerned that their teens learned skills that they had not learned.

What skills do you want your teen to know before they get to be eighteen?

As parents, we must foster and encourage the move to independence in the teenage years, but we must also teach that with increasing independence comes increasing responsibility. Again, I repeat: independence without responsibility produces irresponsible adults.

GOING DEEPER

In the younger years, parents often make decisions on behalf of their children. As kids enter adolescence and begin becoming adults, the parent's role is to help equip their teenagers to start making many of those decisions on their own. Making decisions is how they move toward independence.

Helping a teen move into responsible adulthood requires maintaining an intentional tension between guidance and freedom. As you consider specific areas where you want to help your teen become an adult, below are additional resources to help you on your journey of letting go.

GreenlightCard.com

Most parents struggle with how to teach their kids about money. Most banks won't even let someone get a debit card until their teenage years. *Greenlight* gives parents and kids a shared account where kids can have their own Greenlight card. Parents can monitor it through an app on their phones. Kids have a choice to put their money in three "buckets" on the card: spend, save, or give. It's an easy and helpful way to learn responsibility with finances.

Parenting Teens with Love and Logic: Preparing Adolescents for Responsible Adulthood—by **Foster Cline and Jim Fay**

This popular resource lays out a particular parenting strategy that empowers parents to set limits, teach essential skills, and encourage their teens' decision-making. It begins with clear boundaries, expectations, and consequences, and puts the responsibility for following those expectations back on the teenager. The book and video series are beneficial for parents with strong-willed and rebellious teens.

Houzz and *Pinterest*
—**Room decorating websites and phone apps**

Creating a uniquely personal space is part of growing into independence. One practical way to come alongside your teen is to help guide them in creativity and decision-making. There are countless numbers of home design websites and phone apps, like Houzz and Pinterest, that can help the brainstorming begin. Spending time scrolling through pictures with your child could give you insight into their style preferences and interests.

Adulting 101: #Wisdom4Life—A Complete Guide on Life Planning, Responsibility and Goal Setting
—**by Pete Hardesty and Josh Burnette**

School classrooms rarely teach basic life skills. This book lays out practical steps your teen can take toward independence. It teaches skills like finding employment, buying a car, goal setting, money management, and communicating effectively. There is also a Book 2 in this series that addresses common mental health issues facing adolescents.

Boundaries with Teens: When to Say Yes, How to Say No —by John Townsend

To help teenagers develop into healthy adults, parents must teach them how to take responsibility for their actions, attitudes, and emotions. In this well-known bestseller, Dr. Townsend offers solid principles to help you deal with disrespectful attitudes and set healthy boundaries with your children.

Liturgy of the Ordinary—by Tish Harrison Warren

This award-winning book helps readers look at ordinary things, like making the bed or losing your keys, as "spiritual" practices. Independence is about more than your kids having personal bank accounts. It's also about them developing a spiritual understanding, apart from their parents. *Liturgy of the Ordinary* offers accessible and transformative insight into how you and your teen can both connect with God in the simplest acts of your day.

THINK ABOUT IT

1. What moves toward independence have you observed in your teen or preteen?

2. Reflect on your own teenage years. What efforts did you make to establish your own independence?

3. Have you affirmed or condemned your teen's efforts to express their independence?

4. What responsibilities did you have as a teenager? What skills had you developed by the time you were eighteen?

5. What responsibilities are you already requiring of your teen or preteen? What added responsibilities might you explore?

6. Make a list of all the things you would like for your teen to be able to do by the time they are eighteen. Let the teen help you make the list. Then, discuss which of these can be taught and learned now.

Chapter 5

I Wish I'd Known . . .

That Teens Need to Learn Social Skills

Success in life is greatly impacted by how we relate to people. If teenagers do not learn positive social skills at home, where will they learn them? The reality is that many adults lose jobs, marriages, and mental health because they never learned how to relate to people in a healthy manner. I believe that one of the most important roles of parents is to teach children social skills. Hopefully this began when the children were young. In the teen years we are simply building on the foundation that began in childhood. However, it is never too late to begin. I wish I'd known that helping a teen develop social skills is as important as seeing that they get a good education.

In this chapter, I want to share four social skills that every teen needs to learn. I will seek to focus on practical ways parents can help the teen make these skills a way of life. When these skills become a part of the teen's character, they will enhance the teen's relationships both now and in the future.

THE SKILL OF EXPRESSING GRATITUDE

Gratitude is not genetic. If you hear a teen expressing gratitude, they learned it from someone, most likely their parents. Gratitude is a way of thinking about life. It focuses on what you have, not what you lack. Some teens are known for grumbling about what they don't have: "Everyone in my class has one except me." The grateful teen certainly has desires, but is thankful for what they already have. So, how do we teach teens to replace grumbling with gratitude?

It all begins with the parent's attitude. Are you a grateful parent or a grumbling parent? How do you think your teenager would answer that question? Would you be willing to ask your teen this question: "On a scale of 0 to 10, how would you rank me on being a grateful parent?" One teen responded, "Well, Mom, you are grateful, but you do complain a lot. I would rank you about a 4." His mom was shocked, but she now knows how her son perceives her. We are not likely to teach our teen something we have not yet learned.

One wonderful thing about being human is that we can change our attitude. Once we change the way we think about life, it will be reflected in our words and our behavior. So maybe you could make this a "family project." Have a family conference in which you say something like this: "I have been thinking about how much I have been grumbling lately. I don't like that about me. So, I am going to really work at replacing grumbling with gratitude. Instead of complaining about things, I'm going to start looking for things for which

I can be thankful. For the next three weeks, I'm going to give you permission to call to my attention anytime you hear me grumbling or complaining. When you do, I'll stop and think, and then share two things I am thankful for. Is everyone willing to help me?" Most teens and younger children will sign up for this project. It would be ideal if both parents would be open to the children's help. Habits and attitudes can be changed in three weeks.

At the end of the three weeks, how about another family conference in which parents express appreciation to the children and teens for their help? Then start another three-week project. Each family member who is old enough to write will put the name of other family members at the top of a page, one page for each family member. Every week, write three things you appreciate about that person. Hold a weekly meeting where each of you reads your thoughts aloud to the others. I predict that you will be shocked— and greatly encouraged—by what your teen and other children write about each other and their parents.

Other gratitude-building projects could focus on "things" for which we are thankful. For example, put each family member in a different room or area of the house, and let them list five things in that room for which they are thankful. Another week, everyone could go outside and list five things they appreciate about nature, or five things they appreciate about God. Another idea is an Alphabet of Gratitude, in which each family member is challenged to make a list of things for which they are thankful that begin with each letter of the alphabet.

Once a week at the dinner table, each family member could be asked to share one thing they appreciate about the person to their left or right. Writing a "thank-you" note to a grandparent who has given them a gift or some teacher from their past who impacted their lives helps the teen think of the people and things for which they are grateful. These kinds of family experiences will help build an attitude of gratitude in the heart of the teen. The teenager for whom gratitude becomes a way of life will have a distinct advantage in developing healthy relationships in life.

A freshman college student said, "One of the things I appreciate about my parents is that they taught me to be thankful. So many of my classmates complain about everything. I don't even like to be around them. They are so negative. As my dad always said, 'I see the glass half full, not half empty.' I am so grateful to have the opportunity to be in college. I just want to make the most of these four years. I wake up every morning and thank God that I am alive and have this opportunity." What parent would not like to hear words like this coming from their son or daughter?

THE SKILL OF ASKING QUESTIONS

Asking questions is a social skill that every teen needs. I have always been fascinated that when children are young they are always asking questions, but when they get to be teens, they often become quiet. They may question their parents' ideas or decisions, as we discussed in chapter 1, but seldom ask questions of their peers or other adults whom they encounter. I think this is rooted in the teens' desire to appear competent. Parents often say, "Now that he is a teenager, he thinks he knows everything." I was rummaging through an open market in San Antonio when I saw a plaque with the following words: "Teenagers! Tired of being hassled by your parents? Act now. Move out, get a job, pay your own bills . . . while you still know everything."

Teens want to be respected, admired, and accepted. They think that they must appear competent to reach this goal. They don't want to appear stupid, so they give the appearance that they are intelligent. Inside, they have the same insecurities that you had when you were a teenager. They are trying to compensate for these insecurities. If a parent understands this reality, they will be less condemning of the teen's "know-it-all" attitude.

However, I am not talking about asking questions to gain knowledge. I'm talking about asking questions because you have a genuine interest in getting to know people. These questions grow out of the belief that every individual is a person of worth—that, if I ask questions about their journey, I may learn some "life lessons" I would never discover in the normal flow of life.

Teens will not learn the skill of asking questions unless parents are intentional in teaching and modeling it for them. Do they hear you ask questions of your spouse when you are sharing a family meal? Do you ask the teen's opinion on the topic? What about encouraging each family member to ask the opinion of someone outside the family, on that topic, and report back to the family? If asking questions is an integral part of family life, the teen will likely take the practice to their peers and their teachers.

If your teen expresses an interest in a particular vocation, why not find someone in that vocation and ask if they would be willing to talk with your teen about their vocational journey? Let the teen make a list of possible questions they might ask. Questions such as: "How did you get interested in your vocation? What training did it require? What do you enjoy most about your job? What do you find most challenging? What advice would you give me if I wanted to pursue this vocation?" Most adults are willing to talk about their life, but most teens are not asking questions because they have never developed the social skill of asking questions.

What if you made it easy for your teen to have a conversation with each of his/her grandparents? Again, help them make a list of questions they would like to ask. What was life like when you were a teenager? What did you enjoy most and what was your biggest challenge? What were your parents like when you were a teen? What was it like being the parents of my mom/dad? How were they as a teenager? Then they could ask questions about their vocation, marriage, religion, and other topics. Hopefully this will not be a "one time" conversation, but a way of life when the grandparents and teen spend time together. Most grandparents would be happy to talk about their life journey, if teens expressed an interest.

Help your teen develop a list of questions they could ask their peers. Such questions as:

- Where were you born?
- What is your earliest memory as a child?
- What did you enjoy doing when you were in preschool?
- Where did you attend elementary school?
- Who was your favorite teacher? Who was your worst teacher and why?
- Who is your favorite teacher this year?
- What is your favorite class?
- How would you describe your mother or father?
- Do you have brothers or sisters? What are they like?

- Do you think you will go to college when you finish high school? Where might you like to go?

- What do you think you might like to do when you are an adult?

- Do you attend church?

- Do they have a youth group? What do you enjoy most about the group?

- What is your favorite sport?

- What is your favorite team?

- Do you play a musical instrument?

- What is your favorite song?

Teens who learn to express interest in the lives of other teens will build meaningful friendships, and will develop a relationship skill that will serve them well in the adult world.

From time to time I engage a teenager in the lobby of our church, and ask them some of the questions noted above. They are usually open to give me answers. Often, I sense they are surprised that I would be interested in them. However, seldom does one of these teens ask me questions about my childhood, or my life as a teenager, or questions about my vocation. It is obvious they have not been trained in the skill of asking questions. But again, it is never too late to start.

The teen who learns to ask questions will never meet a stranger who remains a stranger. They will likely build strong friendships and will find this skill a tremendous asset in their vocation. People tend to like people who express interest in them by asking questions. Questions communicate respect and value, something that all humans crave.

THE SKILL OF LISTENING

Hearing and listening are two different things. We hear every sound that hits our eardrums. We hear a siren in the distance. We hear the hum of the air conditioner. Except for the deaf, hearing is simply one of our five senses and requires nothing of us. Listening is a learned skill and requires effort on our part. The teen who learns the social skill of listening when others are talking has a distinct advantage in life. They will likely build healthier relationships and be more successful in their career.

How do parents teach teens this important social skill? As with so many things, it begins with the parents' model. The challenge for some parents is they have never developed this skill themselves. The good news is that we can all learn to become good listeners. So, what are some of the keys in developing this skill?

It starts with valuing other people. If someone is speaking to me, it is because they have something they wish to communicate. They have thoughts and feelings that they want me to understand. If I truly value them as a person, then I will make every effort to give them my full attention. To understand and to be understood is a fundamental building block of good relationships. Once I choose to value the person who is talking, I will be highly motivated to learn the skills of a good listener.

Among those skills, none is more important than giving them my undivided attention. This can be a huge challenge in our distracted world. Think about the last time you were listening to your spouse or your teen. Did you respond to the ping of a text while they were talking? If so, you just communicated that someone "out there" is more important than them. (I understand if you are a medical doctor or someone who is on call 24/7. You can at least say, "I am very interested in what you are saying. Don't leave; let me make sure this is not an emergency.") Most of us will need to break the habit of looking at our screen when someone is talking to us. When you give your teen your undivided attention when they are talking, you are teaching them the social skill of listening.

This same principle applies to other distractions, which we often call multitasking. Certainly you can hear the words of your teen while you are sorting papers on your desk, reading a book, or emptying the dishwasher, but you are not teaching them the skill of effective listening. It is certainly fine to say, "Let me get this in the oven, so I can give you my full attention." Now you are dealing realistically with whatever you were doing when your teen started talking, but you are also communicating that you are interested in what they are saying. Undivided attention implies making eye contact. You are not looking over the teen's head or at the floor when they are talking.

Listen with your neck. Nodding your head indicates, "I'm trying to understand what you are saying. I'm with you." Listen with your back. Lean forward rather than sitting rigidly. A slight forward movement of the body communicates, "You have my full attention." Listen with your feet. Stay put. Don't walk out of the room if your teen says something with which you disagree. Remember, the goal of listening is to understand not only what the other person is thinking, but what they are feeling. Don't interrupt your teen when you disagree with something they are saying. Hear them out. When the teen stops talking, don't give a response, but ask questions to make sure you understood them. "I think I am understanding what you are saying, but let me make sure I'm hearing you correctly. It sounds like you are feeling disappointed that I did not attend your game. Am I correct?"

When the teen feels understood, affirm their thoughts and feelings. "I can see how you would feel disappointed. If I were in your shoes, I probably would feel disappointed also. May I share with you why I had to miss the game?" Because you have affirmed their perspective, they will likely listen to yours. Every time you attentively listen to your teen, you are teaching him/her the social skill of listening.

The kind of listening I am talking about is called by counselors "empathetic listening." It is listening with a view to understanding the thoughts and feelings of the other person, not with a view to responding. It is putting yourself in the shoes of the speaker and trying to see the world through their eyes. Yes, you will eventually give your response, but until you have genuinely heard and affirmed the other person, your response will likely be ill-spoken. Research indicates that the average person listens only seventeen seconds before they interrupt and give a response. Your teen will not feel "heard" if you answer too quickly. Nor will they learn how to listen empathetically.

Why do married adults go to a counselor? Often because they do not feel heard or understood by their spouse. We are not listeners by nature. Our perception is viewed as the right perception in our minds. So we try to convince our spouse to agree with our perception. When we both take this approach, we end up in an argument, often with loud harsh words. Such arguments never lead to understanding.

THE SKILL OF EXTENDING KINDNESS

I define kindness as words or deeds that are designed to help others. What adult does not admire a teen who goes out of her way to help someone else? For the teenager, kindness is more caught than taught. They will observe your kindness to others and likely emulate it. When they are children, you can teach them to express kindness. "Tell your sister how beautiful she looks." "Help Mommy pick up the beans I spilled." "Let's go help Daddy in the yard." "Let's go help Nana by taking her to the grocery store." Again, little children love to help. Often they ask, "Mommy, can I help you?" If they learn the satisfaction of helping others when they are children, they will likely take this social skill into the teen years.

However, when they are teenagers, they tend to become self-absorbed, and may need your model to remind them that helping others is what loving people do. I was walking across the campus of the University of Virginia when I noticed these words etched in stone over one of the doors leading into Cabell Auditorium: "You are here to enrich the world, and you impoverish yourself if you forget the errand." Your teen needs these words engraved on his brain. Maybe it would help if you had them engraved on wood or written on paper and displayed in your house.

Kind words can encourage those to whom they are spoken and bring a feeling of worth to the one who spoke them. Perhaps ask the teen to listen for kind words spoken by others throughout the day and to write them down. You could make it a family game, by asking every family member to do the same and report that night at dinner. The one who has the most will get a prize. In the process of listening for kind words, the teen becomes more thoughtful of speaking kind words.

Recently, I spoke on the topic of "kindness" at my church. Afterward, a teenage girl came up to me and said, "Dr. Chapman, that was a very helpful sermon. It reminded me of how kind my parents are. It also reminded me that I need to focus more on being kind to others. I especially liked the idea of listening to the kind words that I hear others speak each day. I'm going to try to do that this week. I'll write them down and show them to you next week." I thanked her and told her I would look forward to seeing her list. Next Sunday, she showed me her list. It was quite impressive. Some of the comments came from classmates at school and some from her parents and siblings, and one from her grandmother. She said, "This week, I'm going to try to speak some of these words to others." I commended her and said to myself, "What if everyone who heard that sermon would have put it into practice as she did?" Teens and adults need to be reminded of the power of kind words.

But kindness is also expressed in actions. We hear people talk about "random acts of kindness," such as paying for the person's food who is in the car behind you at the drive-through. Such actions leave a lasting impression on the person who is on the receiving end of such kindness. Recently, my wife and I were walking out of a restaurant. When I stopped to pay, the lady said, "Oh, someone has already paid your bill." In shock, I said, "Really? Well, that was nice. In that case, I need to go back to the table and double my tip, so I can feel like I too did an act of kindness."

Kind acts don't always involve money. Teens who open doors for adults as they walk into a building are expressing kindness. Have you taught this simple social skill to your teenager? As they develop this act of kindness, your teen will likely hear positive responses from adults, which will also build their self-esteem.

One way to help teens build acts of kindness into their lifestyle is to play the same observation game we discussed with "kind words." That is, have each family member look for and record acts of kindness observed that day. The one who makes the most observations gets a prize. The more often we observe acts of kindness in others, the more likely we are to develop this social skill.

As in developing most social skills, acts of kindness should begin at home. Have you asked your spouse or teen this question recently: "What can I do to help you today, or this week?" As they hear you asking this question and then following through with some act of kindness, they will likely begin to ask you that question. If not, you may want to have a family conference and discuss the value of doing acts of kindness for each other in the family and to those outside the family. I am convinced that the happiest teen will be the one for whom kindness, in words and deeds, has become a way of life.

GOING DEEPER

Here are more ideas for encouraging kindness in your teen:

Jesus Journey: Shattering the Stained-Glass Superhero and Discovering the Humanity of God—by **Trent Sheppard**

This forty-day devotional is relatable for teenagers but just as impactful for adults. Consider reading it along with your preteen or teenager and discussing how the life of Christ can guide us in our interactions with others.

Practicing the Presence of People: How We Learn to Love
—by Mike Mason

Love is something we must learn. And so are social skills. This book provides philosophical guidance in helping you and your children learn to build deeper, more meaningful relationships with others.

7 Habits of Highly Effective Teens—by Sean Covey

This classic follow-up to *The 7 Habits of Highly Effective People* teaches teenagers necessary social skills like teamwork, listening, resisting peer pressure, building friendships, and responding to bullying. It was recently updated to tackle some of the newer issues of the digital age.

Between Us Girls: Walks and Talks for Moms and Daughters
—by Trish Donohue
Between Us Guys: Life-Changing Conversations for Dads and Sons
—by Joel Fitzpatrick

One of the most essential social skills for your child to develop is learning the art of conversation. The most natural place for them to practice is with their parents. These two resources provide conversation guides for mothers and fathers to engage with kids. While both books are aimed at younger readers (daughters ages seven to fourteen, sons ages six to ten), the questions and topics can be easily adapted depending upon your child's age. Topics range from social justice to friendship to money to anger.

THINK ABOUT IT

1. On a scale of 0–10, how would you rate yourself on these social skills?

   - Expressing gratitude

   - Asking questions

   - Listening

   - Kindness

2. Assuming there is "room for growth," which of these would you like to focus on this week? What steps will you take?

3. Which of these skills do you see most developed in your teen?

   Find an opportunity this week to verbally commend them for what you observe.

4. Which of these skills do you feel is most lacking in your teen? What steps will you take to help develop that skill?

5. Developing social skills does not happen in a week or even a month. However, we can be moving in a positive direction week by week. Remember, acting kindly toward others increases one's sense of self-worth, optimism, and overall satisfaction in life.

Chapter 6

I Wish I'd Known . . .

That Teens Need to Learn How to Process Anger

To be perfectly honest, I wish I'd known how to handle my own anger before we had teenagers. I don't remember having a problem with anger until I got married, and I don't remember having a super problem with anger until we had a teenage son. How about you? I'll share my story later, but first let's try to understand the source of anger. Why do all humans get angry? I believe it is because we are moral creatures. We have a sense of right and wrong. When we encounter what we consider to be "wrong," something inside of us cries out, "This is not right!" With that thought comes the strong emotion of anger.

Think about the last time you experienced anger. Chances are you will discover that, in your mind, someone treated you unfairly or something was not working right. This is why men get angry with lawn mowers. "The thing is not working right!" This is why everyone gets angry with computers or printers. This is why husbands and wives sometimes feel anger toward each other. This is why parents feel angry with their teenager, and why teens often feel angry with their parents. I believe the purpose of anger is to motivate us to seek to right the wrongs we encounter. All great social reform has been born out of anger. People take action seeking to right the wrongs in society.

However, sometimes our efforts make things worse instead of better. People have been known to burn buildings, commit murder, and perform other atrocities under the influence of anger. Husbands and wives have destroyed their marriage by mismanaged anger. Many young single adults have fractured relationships with their parents because someone did or said something in anger. The problem is not anger. The problem is misguided anger, or uncontrolled anger.

What compounds the problem is that there are two kinds of anger. There is what I call *definitive anger*—a wrong has been committed. And there is *distorted anger*—no wrong was committed; we simply did not get our way. Much of our anger in family relationships falls into the latter category. A wife gets angry with her husband because he forgot to pick up the milk on his way home from work. Forgetting is not morally wrong. It is human. A husband gets angry with his wife because she does not load the dishwasher "correctly"—the way he wants it loaded. Parents get angry with the teen because he dyed his hair orange. Teens may get angry with parents who refuse to let them go to the beach with their friends.

Distorted anger is just as real as definitive anger, but we need to learn to distinguish between the two. Definitive anger should always lead us to seek to right the wrong we have encountered by lovingly confronting the person in the wrong. On the other hand, distorted anger should lead us to ask questions and listen empathetically, trying to understand why the person did what they did. We still may not like what they did, but we realize it is a matter of preference, not a moral failure. We must learn to accept each other's humanity. People are different. They will not always do what we want them to do or the way we want them to do it. As we discussed earlier, empathetic listening leads us to understanding and acceptance, even if we don't agree.

If a teen breaks the rules established by the parents, then parents should see that they suffer the consequences of their decision. However, this should be done in a loving, kind, but firm manner, not with harsh words spoken in the heat of anger. We must control our anger and not let anger control our behavior. The purpose is to help them learn from their mistakes, not to condemn them, stimulating feelings of rejection.

LEARNING THE HARD WAY

So, how do we help our teens learn to process anger in a healthy manner? Unfortunately, I learned the hard way. My son was fourteen when he and I got into a heated argument. I don't even remember the issue, but in anger we both lashed out with loud, harsh, critical words at each other. In the midst of our screaming match, he walked out of the room, and slammed the front door as he left the house. When the door slammed, I woke up. "What have I done?" was the question flashing in my mind. "How could I say the things I said to the son I love?" I sat down on the couch and started crying. My wife tried to console me. She said, "I don't know what we are going to do with him. He has got to learn to respect you." But I knew in my heart that I was fully as guilty as he. When my wife left the room, I poured my heart out to God and confessed my failure. I am so glad that God does not demand perfection of His children, and that He will forgive when we confess.

I don't know how long I sat on the couch reflecting on what had happened, but eventually, my son walked back in the front door and I asked if he would join me. He sat down on the gold chair and I said, "I want to apologize to you for the way I talked to you. No father should ever talk to a son the way I talked to you. In my anger, I said some harsh things, and that is not the way I feel about you. I love you very much, and I want to ask you to forgive me." He responded, "Dad, that was not your fault. I started that. I should not have talked to you that way. When I walked up the road, I asked God to forgive me and I want to ask you to forgive me." We both stood weeping and embraced each other.

When we sat down, I said, "Why don't we both try to learn how to control our anger, and not let anger control us. What if, the next time you are angry with me, you say, 'Dad I'm feeling angry, can we talk?' I'll sit down and listen to you and try to understand why you are angry. And, when I'm angry, I will tell you and we can sit down and I will try to explain why I am angry. Let's see if we can learn to talk our way through anger instead of yelling at each other." He agreed, and that was the turning point for both of us. Our plan worked. Or, maybe I should say we worked our plan. We learned how to acknowledge our anger and how to listen to each other. I wish I had learned how to process anger when I was a teenager, but obviously, I did not. The good news is, it is never too late to learn. I'm just glad I learned while my son was still a teenager.

Here are some practical ideas on processing anger in a positive manner. First, *don't try to deny the feeling of anger.* It is a healthy human emotion. It is like a light on the dashboard of a car telling us that something needs attention. Second, take time to *think before you speak.* My mother did tell me when I was a child, "When you are angry, count to ten before you say anything." I think Mom was on the right track, but if you are counting, I'd say you should probably count to at least a hundred before speaking. Give yourself time to cool down.

You might also take a walk while you are counting. After you stop counting, ask yourself: "Is this definitive anger or distorted anger? Did they do something wrong, or did they just not do what I thought they should do?" Either way, we need to process the anger in a positive manner.

Mismanaged anger always makes things worse. If it is distorted anger, the first step is to acknowledge to yourself that you are self-centered like all other humans. You want others to do what you think they ought to do. The teen who is angry at parents because they won't give her permission to go to the beach with her friends for the weekend thinks that her parents are being unfair. So how would the teen who has learned to process distorted anger in a positive way respond? After her walk, she would say to her parents, "I'm sorry that I got angry. It is just that I really wanted to go to the beach and I felt you were being unfair by not letting me go. I know you are my parents, and I need to respect your decisions. Can you help me understand why you made this decision?" Most parents reading this will likely say, "I can't imagine my teen responding like this. It sounds so unrealistic." I fully admit, this is not the way most teens will respond to their anger. Why? Because they have not yet learned to handle anger in a healthy manner.

THE ANGER WE LEARN

But how will they learn, if not from their parents? The fact is that thousands of teens never learn to handle anger in a positive way, and they carry this handicap into adulthood. This will cause struggles in their own marriage, and their own children will likely follow their example. From generation to generation, uncontrolled anger causes severe relationship problems. As parents we have the opportunity to help our teens learn how to process anger in a positive way. If you have not yet learned to process your own anger, maybe you can do what I did and apologize to your teen. This is often the first step in tearing down the wall of hostility between parent and teen.

Where does the parent go from there? If it is distorted anger, you can say to the teen, "I am feeling angry, and I know that what you did is not wrong, but I do want you to know how I feel. When you did or said____, I felt hurt and angry. May I explain why?" Then you explain what you are thinking and feeling. Then ask, "Do you understand what I am saying?" Let them respond, and then say, "I know you have a perspective on this and I am open to hearing your side. I think it would help me if I understood what you are thinking and feeling."

Listen to their response and affirm their thoughts and feelings. "If I were in your shoes, I would probably think and feel the same way you do," is always a true statement. If you were at their stage of life and had their personality, you would likely feel the way they feel. Then you ask, "How do you think we can work this out?" Chances are, you will find the teen open to making changes; or you may change your mind. At any rate, we are looking for a solution, not a war.

If you believe that your spouse, teen, or anyone else has done something morally wrong to you or someone else, then you can follow a similar approach. In this case, you are sharing why you think this was wrong, and asking if you have misunderstood what they said or did. Moral failure calls for apology and forgiveness, which we will discuss more fully in chapter 7. Without apology and forgiveness, the offense sits as an emotional barrier between the two of you. If there is a sincere apology and genuine forgiveness, the barrier is removed and the relationship can go forward. All of us will need to apologize from time to time, because none of us is perfect.

The teen who learns how to process anger in a healthy manner will likely have good relationships as an adult. On the other hand, uncontrolled anger has caused many young adults to lose jobs, destroy marriages, and hurt children. It is worth the time and effort to teach your teen how to manage anger in a positive way.

GOING DEEPER

Anger is a real problem for many teenagers. It can often feel like a sleeping beast that takes over their minds and bodies. To help them navigate the internal violence, it's crucial to address it holistically—from mental, physical, and spiritual angles. When they better understand their anger's psychological, physiological, and spiritual implications, teenagers are more equipped to handle the waves of emotions when they arise. The resources below speak to anger from all of these different angles.

Hurt: Inside the World of Today's Teenagers—by Chap Clark

Anger is a "secondary emotion." We tend to resort to anger to protect ourselves from other vulnerable feelings such as "hurt." In this clinical study from the early 2000s, Dr. Chap Clark presents significant evidence for why teenagers have felt so hurt and abandoned by adults. If you want to understand why your children feel the way they do, let the kids that were interviewed for this book speak on their behalf.

Brave: A Teen Girl's Guide to Beating Worry and Anxiety —by Sissy Goff

Anger isn't the only emotion with which your teenager is wrestling. According to the National Institutes of Health, nearly one in three adolescents ages thirteen to eighteen will experience an anxiety disorder. This guide, created for girls in that exact age range, helps young ladies understand the roots of anxiety and why the brain is often working against them when they start to worry. Through real-life stories, journaling, and drawing prompts, girls will learn practical ways to fight back when worries arise.

IJM.org—The International Justice Mission

When teenagers experience anger, it is often the result of perceived injustice. It can be helpful to teach kids how to channel anger against actual injustices. One way to do that is by exposing your teenagers to organizations that fight corruption. The International Justice Mission is a global organization that protects people in poverty from violence. They work in fourteen countries to combat trafficking and slavery, violence against women and children, and police abuse of power.

PreemptiveLove.org

Preemptive Love is another organization that strives to bring peace where there is chaos. They show up on the front-lines in places of war and conflict to provide food, shelter, and medical care for those in need. When teenagers catch a vision of the great need in the world, the things they typically get angry about often grow smaller in significance.

Punching bags

There may be debate over the value of including a punching bag when suggesting an appropriate response to teenage anger, but this is a common recommendation for adolescents in therapy. Kids often experience intense emotions with limited outlets. Physical exercise such as weight lifting, running, punching bags, or even yelling into a pillow are much more preferable than many of the behaviors you may have seen. It isn't how we want them to resolve their problems in the longterm, but if you are desperate and need a transitional emotion-management system, a punching bag is much cheaper than replacing the sheetrock in your walls.

THINK ABOUT IT

1. When you were a teenager, did your parents try to teach you how to handle anger? If so, how effective were their efforts? More to the point, how did *they* handle anger?

2. How well are you doing handling your own anger toward people in your life?

3. When is the last time you observed your teenager losing control of his/her anger? What was your response? Do you feel good about your response?

4. Would you be willing to invite your teen to tell you when they are feeling angry? Share that you know all of us get angry and you want them to know that you are willing to listen to their concerns.

5. What is the next step you think you need to take in helping your teen learn how to process anger in a healthy manner?

Chapter 7

I Wish I'd Known . . .

That Teens Need to Learn How to Apologize and Forgive

Teenagers will never be perfect; nor will parents. We don't need to be perfect in order to have good relationships. Aren't we glad for that? However, we do need to deal effectively with our failures. This involves apologizing and forgiving. The adult who does not apologize will likely leave a trail of broken relationships. So, it is extremely important to make sure that your teen knows how to apologize when they wrong someone and how to forgive when others offend them.

Most parents begin this process when their children are young. Little Henry kicks down the block tower his sister has built in her bedroom. His mother says, "Henry, that was wrong. Go tell your sister that you are sorry and ask her to forgive you." Hopefully, little Henry will say, "I'm sorry. Will you forgive me?" Even if he is not sincere, he is beginning to understand that when we mistreat others, we need to apologize. Mom may also ask his sister to forgive him. Sister will not be happy, but she may say, "I forgive you." Again, these are the elementary steps toward teaching children to apologize and forgive.

However, there is much more to be learned about apologizing and forgiving. The teen years provide time for the parent to build on the foundation laid in childhood. Several years ago, I did extensive research on how people apologize, and wrote a book, with my coauthor, Dr. Jennifer Thomas, entitled *When Sorry Isn't Enough.* We asked thousands of people two questions: "When you apologize, what do you say or do? When someone is apologizing to you, what do you want to hear them say or do?" Their answers fell into five categories, and we called them the "five languages of apology." We discovered that people have very different ideas on what a sincere apology looks like. When someone is apologizing to us, we judge their sincerity based on our own idea of a sincere apology. That is why some apologies seem rather lame to us and we find it hard to forgive.

Understanding the five apology languages will equip parents with a tool for teaching their teen how to apologize effectively. Here is a brief summary of the five languages of apology.

1. **Expressing Regret:** This is often done with the words "I'm sorry." However, we should never stop with these two words. Tell them what you are sorry for. "I'm sorry that I lost my temper and yelled at you." "I'm sorry that I made fun of your

new dress." If you only say, "I'm sorry," the offended person may be thinking, "You certainly are." What they want to know is: "Do you really regret what you did? Do you understand how deeply you hurt me? Do you feel pain because of what you did?" When you state your offense, they are more likely to believe that you are sincere.

One of the mistakes that we often make is to add the word "but" after our apology. "I'm sorry that I lost my temper, but if you had not . . . then I would not . . . " Now you are no longer apologizing. You are blaming them for your bad behavior. How do you break this habit of adding the "but"? The next time you hear yourself say, "I'm sorry that I last my temper and yelled at you, but . . . " pause and then say, "Excuse me. Erase the 'but.' I'm sorry that I lost my temper and yelled at you." About the third time you "erase the but," you will have broken this habit.

Avoid the habit of saying, "I'm sorry if what I said offended you." This is not an apology. You are blaming the other person for being offended. My coauthor started recording public apologies made by civic leaders that she heard on television or read in the newspaper. This was one of the most common statements she observed. Apparently, their parents never taught them how to express true regret.

2. **Accepting Responsibility:** "I was wrong. I should not have done that." By nature, teens do not accept responsibility for their behavior if they think it displeased their parents. A teen says, "I didn't buy the cigarettes. Corey bought them and asked

me to just try it. That's all I did, just one puff." In reality he has the pack of cigarettes in his coat pocket. Admitting that they were wrong is hard for some teens because they fear the consequences, but it needs to be a part of a sincere apology. Incidentally, this should be the first step in teaching young children how to apologize. I remember when my son was six or seven years old. We were in the kitchen together and he accidentally knocked a glass off the table. It hit the floor and broke. I turned and looked at him and he said, "It did it by itself!" I said, "Let's say that a different way. 'I accidentally knocked the glass off the table.'" He said with tears, "I accidentally knocked the glass off the table." He did nothing deserving punishment. I was simply trying to help him accept responsibility for his actions.

Some adults find it hard to say, "I was wrong. I should not have done that." Often these are adults who in childhood or in the teen years were verbally abused by their parents. Such statements as, "You don't ever do anything right," still ring in their adult ears. Somewhere in their psyche as they grew up they said to themselves, "When I get to be an adult, I will never be wrong again." They find it hard to admit that they have done anything wrong, for to do so says, "My parents were right—I can't ever do anything right." Parents need to help teens understand that admitting that you were wrong is a sign of strength, not a sign of weakness. Accepting responsibility for our own poor behavior is an important part of a sincere apology.

3. **Offering to make restitution**: "What can I do to make this right? How can I make this up to you? I know I've hurt you, and

I feel badly." This apology speaks loudly to many people. "I'm sorry and I was wrong," is not enough. They want to know what you are going to do to correct the situation. Usually, they will have an idea of what you should do. As a parent, have you ever offered to make restitution to someone whom you have treated badly? Have you ever said to your spouse, "Honey, I know I was wrong. I feel bad about it. How can I make things right with you?" For some people, if you don't offer to "make things right," you have not truly apologized.

Teens need to learn this apology language. Suppose you and your teen get lunch at a fast-food drive-through. He eats his lunch as you drive down the road. When he finishes, he tosses the bag with the trash out the window of the car. What are you going to do? Some parents will lash out in anger and say, "Don't do that. You know that is wrong." If that is all that happens, the teen may say, "I'm sorry." Or he may simply shrug it off without comment. However, if the parent says calmly, "You do know that is against the law, right? In fact, there is a hundred-dollar fine if you are caught dumping trash. So we are going home and get a trash bag and I am going to bring you back and let you pick up your trash. When we do wrong, we need to make things right."

4. **Expressing the desire to change:** "I don't like what I did. I don't want to do that again. Can you help me take steps so I won't do that again?" A teen says to his dad, "Yes, I took ten dollars out of your billfold. I know it was wrong. I am not making excuses. I actually did it once before and didn't get caught. It has bothered me ever since. I don't ever want to do

that again. Can you help me?" A loving dad will have a suggestion. Perhaps he will say, "In the future, what if you just ask me if there is a job you could do for me to earn ten dollars? I will usually have an idea. Or, sometimes I might just give it to you if I think you will use it wisely." He might also add, "I will forgive you because I believe you are sincere, but to make you feel better, would you rake the leaves in the backyard to repay me for the ten dollars?" With this last statement he is teaching the concept of making restitution, after sharing a plan so that his son is not likely to repeat this offense.

5. **Requesting forgiveness:** "Will you forgive me? I love you and I'm sorry that I hurt you. I hope you will forgive me." This opens the door for the offended person to forgive you. We cannot force someone to forgive us, but we can request forgiveness. Some may ask, "Why do I have to ask for forgiveness? Don't they know if I am apologizing that I want to be forgiven?" Perhaps, but for some people requesting forgiveness is part of a sincere apology. When you ask someone to forgive you, it is acknowledging that you know you have put a barrier between you and them by your offense, and that it will not be removed until they forgive you.

The teen who learns to speak all five apology languages will likely grow up to have good relationships. When he speaks all five languages, he will effectively communicate his sincerity. So, how do parents teach the teen to apologize? By speaking all five apology languages to your spouse, your teen, and other people whom you may mistreat. Most of us did not learn to speak these apology languages when we were teens. Our parents may have taught us one or two of these, and those are the ones we naturally speak when we need to apologize. The good news is that you can learn to speak these languages as an adult. Yes, it will seem unnatural the first time you try, but it becomes easier each time you speak it.

After you begin the process of verbalizing each of the languages, your teens will notice that they are hearing things they have never heard before. Then you can have a family discussion on how to apologize effectively, in which you share the five apology languages and let each family member say them aloud to the rest of the family—a trial run getting us ready for when we need to apologize. It will become somewhat of a game, and will likely be done with a bit of humor, but the teen is learning an essential skill in building positive relationships.

In our research, we discovered that about 10 percent of the adult population never apologizes for anything; most of these were men. They learned this from their fathers who said, "Real men don't apologize." Wrong. Real men *do* apologize. In fact, if they don't learn to apologize, they will not have healthy relationships. Don't let your teen become an adult who has this attitude. Real men and women recognize that they are not perfect and are willing to admit it.

FORGIVENESS

Apology alone does not restore relationships. There must be a response to an apology. The response that allows the relationship to go forward is forgiveness. Forgiveness is the decision to pardon the offender—to remove the barrier that the offense created between the two of you. When we have been hurt deeply, it may be difficult to forgive. Our sense of justice pushes us to make them pay for what they did. Our sense of compassion pushes us to choose mercy over justice. In society, justice demands that criminals suffer the consequences of their behavior. That is one of the roles of civil government. However, in personal relationships, it is mercy that allows reconciliation. When there is a sincere apology and genuine forgiveness, the relationship can be restored. Many family relationships are fractured for lack of an apology or refusal to forgive. The teen who learns to forgive will be freed from resentment, stored anger, and hatred—all of which have negative physical and emotional consequences. Forgiveness enhances physical and mental health.

Forgiveness is not a feeling. It is a decision. In our hurt, we may think that forgiveness makes it too easy for the offender. However, when we refuse to forgive, the relationship cannot move forward. The emotional barrier that was created by the offense remains in place. We are estranged emotionally and it will show up in our behavior. By failing to forgive, we are moving away from the person rather than moving toward them. When we fail to forgive our friend or spouse who has apologized, we are making a decision to halt our forward progress. I know that it may take some time to work through the pain when we have been mistreated, but at some juncture, we must make the decision to forgive and move forward or refuse to forgive and settle for a fractured relationship.

There are some things that forgiveness does not do. It does not destroy our memory. You may have heard people say, "If you have not forgotten, you have not forgiven." That is not true. Everything that has ever happened to us is stored in the human brain. From time to time it will jump from the subconscious mind to the conscious mind. You will remember the details of what happened. Vivid images of what they did will roll through your mind, and their hurtful words will ring in your ears. You cannot keep such memories from coming to mind. However, you need not be obsessed with such memories. You remind yourself, "Yes, it did happen and it was bad, but I have chosen to forgive. Now I want to focus on rebuilding our relationship."

With the memories often come strong emotions such as hurt, anger, and disappointment. Forgiveness does not destroy our emotions. When memories and emotions return after they have apologized and you have chosen to forgive, don't try to ignore them. Rather, take them to God and tell Him what you are remembering and feeling. You might say, "Lord, You know what I am remembering today and what I am feeling. But I thank You that I have forgiven them. Now, help me not to allow the memory and emotions to control my behavior. Help me to do something good today." Then you reach out to express love to the person you have forgiven. Your love stimulates their love and the relationship moves forward.

Forgiveness does not rebuild trust. I first discovered this in counseling couples when one of them had been sexually unfaithful. They had broken off the relationship and had sincerely apologized. The spouse had chosen to forgive them. However, in my office, the offended spouse will say, "I have forgiven him/her, but to be honest, I don't trust him/her." Forgiveness does not restore trust. Trust must be earned by being trustworthy. So I say to the partner who apologized, "If you want to be trusted, let your life be an open book. Allow your spouse full access to your computer, smartphone, and every other aspect of your life." Your attitude should be, "My life is an open book. I have hurt you deeply. I am through with deceit." If you take this approach, your spouse will come to trust you again in due time.

What forgiveness does is open the door to the possibility that trust can be reborn. If your teen lies to you about skipping school and going to the lake with friends, his/her apology will not rebuild your trust. Trust comes in time, as they show themselves to be trustworthy. This is a reality that adults and teens need to learn.

What forgiveness doesn't do

Forgiveness does not remove all the consequences of wrongdoing. Perhaps your teen chooses to drive under the influence of drugs or alcohol, and has an accident. He can apologize and you can forgive, but the car is still wrecked, and perhaps people have broken bones or worse. Letting teens suffer the consequences of their behavior is a part of their education. Many parents try to help their teen by removing the consequences. I have seen parents immediately buy the teen a new car, pay for the traffic ticket the teen received for driving under the influence, and remove all other consequences of the teen's misbehavior. In my opinion, this is a serious mistake. We love them and we forgive them, but we let them experience the reality of wrong behavior. Experience is sometimes a hard but effective teacher. One teen said to me, "After spending three nights in jail, I was sobered up and realized what a foolish thing I had done. I decided right then that I would never drink and drive again."

One other reality is, we cannot force someone to forgive us when we have offended them. We can apologize, but we must give them the freedom to choose to forgive or not to forgive. As noted above, we must give them time to process their emotions. If they have been hurt deeply, it may take time for them to be ready to genuinely extend forgiveness. Never condemn them for not forgiving you immediately.

Sometimes we are wronged by a family member or someone

else and they do not apologize. What should we do then? As mentioned earlier, I believe we lovingly confront them and thus open the door for them to apologize. We cannot make them apologize, but we can let them know that what they did has hurt us deeply. If they value the relationship, in time they will likely apologize. Then we can genuinely extend forgiveness. Reconciliation comes only after there has been a sincere apology and a clear decision to forgive.

In teaching your teen to apologize and forgive, your model is fully as important as your instruction. Some parents have said to me, "If I apologize to my teen, won't they lose respect for me?" The answer is no. They will *gain* respect for you. They already know that what you did was wrong. Your apology speaks loudly to them about what to do when they do wrong. Conversely, your forgiveness when your teen apologizes to you teaches him/her how to forgive others. If your teen learns how to apologize and forgive, they are taking with them into adulthood one of the essentials to having good relationships.

GO DEEPER

We have all hurt people. Our sin can be a great source of shame that leads us further into isolation. To bring healing and unity to relationships, we have to work toward becoming better apologizers and forgivers. And this is hard work, but it's a good work.

One of the most influential motivators in our lives is the power of story. If we want to move toward reconciliation, hearing stories of others' courage can be an impactful source of hope. Below is a list of stories and resources that display the power of forgiveness.

Les Miserables—by Victor Hugo

One of the most well-known forgiveness stories of all time is also one of the longest novels in history. If you don't want to tackle the 1,500+ pages, consider watching the 1998 film of the same name, starring Liam Neeson. Watching and discussing meaningful movies with your teenagers can become a significant source of bonding in your relationship.

Fire Road: The Napalm Girl's Journey through the Horrors of War to Faith, Forgiveness, and Peace—by Kim Phuc Pham Thi

In the 1970s, "the napalm girl" was exposed in a photo that made headlines around the world. Her picture has long since defined the horrors of war. If you search the internet for "Fire Road," you will find videos, articles, and an autobiography that tells Kim's powerful journey of faith and forgiveness. It will undoubtedly impact your teenage children.

Redeeming Love—by Francine Rivers

This is one of the less familiar Bible stories but has a strong message about forgiveness, which comes to life in Francine Rivers's dramatic retelling.

Forgiving What You Can't Forget: Discover How to Move On, Make Peace with Painful Memories, and Create a Life That's Beautiful Again—by Lysa TerKeurst

Lysa TerKeurst is a survivor of major betrayal. She tells her story of hope and healing in this book, as well as on her *Proverbs 31 Ministries* podcast. You can find more of her resources for forgiveness at LysaTerkeurst.com.

The 5 Apology Languages: The Secret to Healthy Relationships
(formerly titled *When Sorry Isn't Enough*)
—by Gary Chapman and Jennifer Thomas

If you feel like it's too late for restoration with someone close to you, this is a step-by-step guide for mending broken relationships. It will help you better understand how to both give and receive forgiveness.

THINK ABOUT IT

1. How well have you learned to apologize? Can you remember the last time you apologized to anyone? How did that work out? Is there someone to whom you need to apologize?

2. What did your parents teach you about apology when you were a teen? What do you wish they had done differently?

3. What have you intentionally or unintentionally taught your teen about apologies? When is the last time you heard them apologize to you or someone else?

4. Would you be open to giving your teen (or each family member) a copy of *The 5 Languages of Apology*, and discussing them in a family meeting?

5. Is there someone who has apologized to you, but you have not yet chosen to forgive them? What would it take for you to make the decision to forgive?

6. Is there anyone who has hurt you and has not apologized? Have you lovingly confronted them with your hurt and thus opened the door for them to apologize?

Chapter 8

I Wish I'd Known . . .
That Teens Need Guidance

I knew that children could not survive without guidance. I also knew that parents were typically the primary guides for their children. One of the saddest things I have encountered in my counseling has been parents who abdicate this parental role, either through absence or abuse. So I was committed to being involved in giving my children guidance. What I did not expect was that, in the teen years, the need for parental guidance would increase. Before a child turns thirteen, the options for making poor decisions are somewhat limited. The child lives within certain parameters established by the parents. However, in the teen years the world of opportunities explodes. The possibilities of making life-altering decisions increase.

Some of these decisions are positive. Our daughter decided early on that she wanted to be a medical doctor. So, in high school, she took four years of Latin and multiple science courses. This prepared her well for a premed major in college. However, some decisions made by teens are not so good. Yes, teens need even more parental guidance than when they were children. What we want as parents is for our teens to reach their potential for good in the world, both during the teen years and later as adults. Parental guidance plays a key role in helping this dream become a reality.

The goal is not to control our teen's decisions; that is, make decisions for them. Our goal is to help *them* make wise decisions. While we hear a lot about peer pressure, research clearly indicates that parental influence is the greatest influence on the teen's decisions. Whether this influence is positive or negative depends on two things: the parent-teen relationship, and the moral character of the parent. If parents have not lived up to their own moral beliefs, the teen is less likely to listen to their advice. The greater the gap between what parents say they believe and how they actually live, the more difficult it is for the teen to respect the parents. For these parents, the starting point is a sincere apology and a change in their past behavior patterns, which we discussed in chapter 7.

LOVING, MODELING, TEACHING

Assuming that parents are emotionally, mentally, and spiritually healthy, the focus needs to be on building a loving relationship with the teenager. If the teen feels deeply loved by the parents, he/she is strongly influenced by the parents' model and advice. When the teen believes that the parents want what is best for the teen and are not simply trying to force their own preferences on the teen, it is easier to comply with the parents' requests or suggestions. Learning and speaking the teen's primary love language consistently, as we discussed in chapter 3, will go a long way toward creating an emotional bond between parent and teen. The social skills of asking questions and listening empathically, which we discussed in chapter 5, will help the teen feel valued, understood, and respected.

Parental guidance involves trying to model and teach the teen to make wise decisions. The underlying reality is that every decision has consequences. Each of us must live with the results of our own decisions. The depth of this reality has not deeply penetrated the mind of most teenagers. Teens tend to live for the moment. If it looks like fun, if their friends are doing it, then "why not give it a try?" is the attitude of many teens.

Parents may use their own poor decisions to demonstrate the reality of consequences. I remember a father who had lung cancer, saying to his teenage son: "One of my deepest regrets is that when I was fourteen years old, I started smoking cigarettes. I have lung cancer because I made that decision. I hope you will be wiser than I was when I was a teenager." His son said, "Dad, I know that when you were young, people did not know that smoking tobacco caused lung cancer. Now we know. You don't have to worry about me using tobacco products. I love you, Dad." The father told me, "That's a conversation I will never forget." Teens can learn by observing the poor choices made by parents, but the message is much more powerful when the parent acknowledges their wrong decisions.

Parents can also influence their teens by drawing attention to the painful results of bad decisions made by other teenagers. Sharing an article about someone getting killed in an automobile accident because a teen was driving under the influence of alcohol or drugs can be sobering to your teenager. Don't preach to them. Just say, "I thought you might want to read this. It is really sad. Can you imagine how that young man must feel?" Or, if you are watching the news on television with your teen and see a story about a bad accident or even criminal behavior, you might simply say: "That makes me want to cry. That one decision has ruined his life forever." You don't have to pontificate about how foolish the young man was, nor warn your son or daughter to never do such a thing. They got the message without your sermon.

THE DANGER OF "GIVE IT A TRY"

In our contemporary world, one area in which teens will need parental guidance is in responding to the appeal of opioids, alcohol, marijuana, smoking, and vaping. Many of their peers will urge them to "give it a try." The research is clear: most adults who are addicted to alcohol or drugs began when they were teenagers. They did not intend to become addicts. They just wanted to have fun. I have never met an adult who chose not to use alcohol or drugs when they were a teenager who ever regretted their decision. I have met hundreds of adults who chose to "give it a try" when they were teenagers who deeply regret their decision.

Perhaps you could give your teen a challenge to do a little research project for you. Remember, researchers get paid, so offer them an hourly wage if they will Google the negative effects of specific drugs—marijuana, cocaine, opioids—and give you a report. Or, you could ask them to do research and you will do the same and see who can find the most information on the subject. Thirteen would be the ideal time to do this project. The sooner the teen is exposed to the truth, the more likely he is to make a wise decision.

You might also want to Google and find out how many people were killed in automobile accidents last year because of someone driving under the influence of drugs or alcohol.

Obviously, parents differ in their own views of alcohol and drugs. Some parents are addicts themselves. Others drink or smoke in moderation. One question to ask is: Do you want your teen to follow your example? If your answer is "Yes," then you will likely influence them in that direction. If your answer is "No," then perhaps the place to begin is to change your own behavior.

I have always sought to encourage teens not to use drugs, alcohol, or tobacco until they are twenty-five years old. This is based on research that clearly indicates that the human brain is not fully developed until the age of twenty-five. If a person follows this plan, they will likely make a wise decision when they are twenty-five. Why would you want to mess up your brain before it is fully developed? A healthy brain is a great asset in high school, college, and as you start your career.

TEENS, SEX, AND GUIDANCE

Hopefully sex education began in the home long before the child became a teenager. If so, then the parent is simply building on that foundation. However, in the teen years, parents must not ignore this topic. The voices of modern culture regarding sexuality are extremely distorted. The teen desperately needs your influence in this area. Some parents find this difficult because they don't know where to begin. If you have welcomed the teen's questions on other topics, they will probably ask questions related to sex. This is the most natural entree to talking about sex. However, if the teen does not ask questions, the parent must be proactive and turn the teen's attention to the topic.

One of the easiest ways to do this is to give the teen a book that deals with sexuality in a manner that is consistent with your own views (which means you must read the book first). Ask the teen to read it and let you know if they find it helpful. This is a non-threatening way to open discussion.

If you have a teenage son, I would also recommend a book I wrote with Dr. Clarence Shuler entitled: *Choose Greatness: 11 Wise Decisions That Brave Young Men Make*. This book deals not only with sexuality but with ten other topics. If a father and son read the chapters and discuss the questions at the end of each chapter, it can be a helpful avenue for meaningful communication. This book can be ordered at moodypublishers.com.

Helping teens make wise decisions related to sexuality is extremely important. One of the sad things I deal with in my counseling office is listening to parents share that their teenage daughter is pregnant, or their son has a sexually transmitted disease. Your teen needs your guidance in understanding sexuality. Open conversations on this topic can help the teen make wise decisions. I know that we cannot control our teens' behavior, but we can help them understand that every decision we make has consequences. Getting a clear picture of this reality can help them choose wisely.

RESPECT

Teens need guidance in respecting adults, especially those with whom they interact such as schoolteachers, coaches, grandparents, and school bus drivers. Many teachers complain that their biggest problem is the disrespect they experience from students. Simply maintaining order in the classroom is a major challenge. Coaches tend to get more respect, perhaps because students know if they don't follow instructions, they will be kicked off the team. Many school bus drivers are also coming to report students to parents and school principals when there is disruptive behavior on the bus. A growing number of grandparents are saying, "I can't believe how my grandchildren ignore rules when they come to my house. It makes me reluctant to have them over. "

Of course there are teachers, coaches, faith leaders, and others who abuse their authority, sometimes with devastating consequences. Still, we cannot overlook those good servants who are in these positions because they genuinely want to help people.

Why have we seen this growth in disrespect in our culture? I believe that much of it can be traced back to parents who have failed to give guidance. Absentee fathers or abusive fathers have left young men without a model of respect. Many of these teens are filled with anger because they feel unloved and rejected. Their disrespect for authority is their way of expressing their anger. I am deeply empathetic with single mothers who are raising teens without the help of the teen's father. I would urge these mothers to make every attempt to find a trusted male who might serve as a substitute father for these young men. I would also urge involvement in a local church or civic organization that provides classes for children and teenagers. Learning to show respect for everyone we encounter is rooted in the belief that all humans are of equal value. Respecting others as you would want to be respected is a lesson that needs to be learned by all teenagers.

Again, how are you, the parent, modeling respect for others? When parents make derogatory comments about people of a different race or culture, or about people in certain vocations, it gives the teen the freedom to do the same. We are all greatly influenced by the family in which we grew up and the culture in which we live. Thus, from our history we may have developed negative attitudes toward certain groups of people. As adults, we must evaluate the attitudes developed in our past. Such evaluation may well lead us to change our thinking and thus our treatment of others.

Another way we teach respect is to verbally correct our teen when we hear him/her expressing disrespect for their mother, father, or some other family member. The message the teen needs to hear is, "Every member of our family is important. We will treat each other with respect." Appropriate consequences must be administered when a teen fails to do so. When we have this kind of family atmosphere, the teen is getting the first and most basic lesson in showing respect.

If and when the parent learns that a teen has been disrespectful of a teacher or anyone else, the same loving but firm action should be taken. The message needs to be clear: "That is not the way we treat people." By nature, adults and teens are self-centered. We tend to be judgmental of others who are unlike us. We don't want others telling us what to do. When we feel others are trying to control us, we rebel. Such rebellion often leads to behavior that hurts both the other person and ourselves. Learning to control anger and speaking with kindness and honesty to the person who has offended us is far more likely to lead to a satisfactory resolution of the issues. Growing in the challenge of respecting others is important for adults and teens.

In the book *Choose Greatness: 11 Wise Decisions That Brave Young Men Make*, mentioned above, we acknowledge that there are scores of decisions a teenager will make, each of which will make their life better or worse. We give twelve questions for the teen to ask himself/herself before making a decision. I list them here with the thought that parents may want to share them with their teenagers.

Will this have a negative or positive effect on my health?

How will this impact my ability to think clearly?

How will this decision impact my parents or other adults who care for me?

Is this decision unlawful?

Is this decision morally right or wrong?

How will this decision impact my siblings?

Am I being influenced by others to do something I really don't want to do?

Will I stand up for what I know is right rather than give in to the pressure of others?

How will this decision affect my future education?

Is this decision consistent with what I believe about God?

Will I be glad that I made this decision five years from now?

Does this decision help me become the person I want to be?

Teenagers need guidance, and no one is more influential than parents in helping them make wise decisions. If the teen makes poor decisions, as parents we love them, but also allow them to suffer the consequences of their decisions. Sometimes experience is the best teacher. The teen who learns to make wise decisions will most likely make wise decisions as an adult.

GOING DEEPER

It's been said that "whoever tells the best story wins." In order for parents to guide their children through difficult decisions, it's crucial to frame that guidance in a positive light. While it's easier to communicate what you're against, it takes more intentionality to explain what you are for. The resources below provide helpful direction.

Love Thy Body: Answering Hard Questions about Life & Sexuality—by Nancy Pearcey

Love Thy Body doesn't shy away from some of the most difficult questions of our day. It tackles the issues of gender identity, hookup culture, abortion, sexuality, and more.

Fearfully and Wonderfully: The Marvel of Bearing God's Image —by Philip Yancey and Dr. Paul Brand

This is a fascinating read that will reawaken the wonder and mystery of God's thumbprint on the human body. If your teenager is interested in science, anatomy, or the medical field, this book will be a fantastic conversation starter—and teens will be interested in Dr. Brand's work helping those with leprosy.

The Wisdom Pyramid: Feeding Your Soul in a Post-Truth World —by Brett McCracken

The Wisdom Pyramid shines a light on the harmful and addictive streams of information constantly vying for teens' attention. McCracken offers a clear path to help both adults and children moderate their media consumption and find more reliable methods of gaining true wisdom.

THINK ABOUT IT

1. What kind of influence did your parents have on the decisions you made as a teenager? In what ways would you like to emulate your parents? In what ways would you like to be different?

2. To what degree do you think you have a healthy relationship with your teen? What steps could you take to enhance the relationship?

3. Do you know and speak your teen's primary love language consistently?

4. Do you give your teen your full attention when they want to talk? Have you learned to affirm their thoughts and feelings even when you disagree with them?

5. In what area do you feel your teen most needs your guidance at his/her present age?

6. What in this chapter have you found most helpful?

Chapter 9

I Wish I'd Known . . .

That Teens Need to Learn an Attitude of Service

I walked into the lobby of my local bank and the teller said with a smile, "How may I help you today?" "Just a simple deposit," I said. She took care of the transaction and said, "Have a good afternoon." "Same to you," I said. From there I drove to the local post office to mail a package. I stood in line, awaiting my turn, and finally stood before the attendant—who said nothing. "I need to mail this package," I said. Still he said nothing as he took the package and weighed it. "Nine-seventy six," he said. I gave him a ten and he gave me the change. I said, "Thank you," and he nodded. I didn't know if it was company policy that accounted for the difference in those two encounters, or if one of them had a parent who taught the joy of serving others while the other did not. But I knew which one I wanted my teenager to emulate.

One of life's greatest joys is found in serving others. Albert Schweitzer was a medical doctor who chose to invest his life not in making money, but in going to Africa and helping those who had little access to medical care. Near the end of his life he received the Nobel Peace Prize. He is attributed with saying that "the only ones among you who will be really happy are those who will have sought and found how to serve." He spoke with the voice of experience. It has been my observation that those who live self-centered lives seldom find true happiness, while those who choose an attitude of service to others find deep satisfaction.

Many people will agree that Jesus of Nazareth made the greatest positive impact of anyone in history. If you read the story of His life, you will discover that it was a life dedicated to serving others. He said of Himself, " . . . the Son of Man did not come to be served, but to serve . . ."[1] He instructed His followers: "As I have loved you, so you must love one another."[2]

To the degree that His followers emulate His lifestyle, they too will make a positive impact on the world. History is replete with examples of this. Thousands of educational institutions, hospitals, orphanages, and other philanthropic organizations found their birth in the hearts of men and women who had an attitude of service to others.

Children are not born with this attitude. We are by nature self-centered. If we are left to our own natural instincts, we will look out for ourselves and hope that others do the same. However, if we have an attitude of service, we will certainly take care of our own needs, but our driving force will be to help others. Such a lifestyle may lead to wealth, rank, and honor, but these too will be turned toward serving others. On the other hand, those who choose a lifestyle of service may never accumulate wealth or position. They realize that life's true meaning is not found in these things, but in investing one's life in serving others.

BEING A GIVER, NOT A TAKER

So how do parents help teens develop an attitude of service? There is no magic wand or secret formula, but I believe parents must first be convinced that they want to personally leave the world a better place than they found it. They want to be "givers" rather than "takers." If this is the attitude of parents, then they will want to raise children who are committed to the same attitude. An attitude of service is more caught than taught. In my own teen years, I remember my dad mowing grass for neighbors when they were sick, and taking food from our garden to those who were in need. I remember my mom cooking meals and taking them to others. I don't remember them ever telling me that I should serve others, but somewhere along the line, I got the picture.

"What can I do to help you?" is a question that should be asked in any family who wants to have teens who seek to serve others. Mom is asking this question to Dad, and Dad is asking the question to Mom. They are both asking the question to their teenagers. I predict that in due time the teen will begin asking the question of their parents. Developing an attitude of service begins in the home. In many ways, moms and dads are already serving their children and each other. It may be out of a sense of duty or out of a sense of love, but without some level of service to other family members, the family cannot survive. Remember, love itself is an attitude, not a feeling. Service is but an expression of love. Love is the attitude that says to oneself, "I want to enrich the lives of my family and those outside my family. I want to make the world a better place." Asking the questions "What can I do to help you?" or, "How may I help you?" is one way of keeping service on the front burner of family members.

Recruiting your teen to help you in service projects outside the home is another way of helping them discover the satisfaction of helping others. One of the projects I did when our children were teens was to take them with me in the fall to rake the leaves of elderly neighbors who were no longer able to rake their own leaves. I remember our daughter saying, "Dad, it feels so good to help older people." It is experiences like this that lead teens later to help people their own age at school. A parent recently shared with me that once a month they were taking their teen with them to help at the local food pantry on Saturday mornings. They would prepare food boxes that were delivered in the afternoon. Teens who learn the joy of helping others will likely make it a way of life when they are adults.

Teaching teens an attitude of service is preparing them to make the most of their vocation. Adults who see their career as a way of helping people will find much more satisfaction in their work. Some vocations such as schoolteachers, doctors, nurses, and many others are clearly service-oriented. In fact, most vocations in some way serve others, but many people are thinking of their vocation as simply a means of providing for their family financially. If they have an attitude of service, they will focus on how their job is helping others and will find a much deeper sense of satisfaction about their work. It will not simply be a job. It will be a vocation, which means "a calling" or "a mission."

I met a lady some time ago who worked in a blanket factory. Her job was sewing the hem at the top of the blanket. Day after day, that is what she did. I asked if she ever got bored with her work. She replied, "No, because I know that every blanket I hem will someday keep someone warm. I love my job." She was a lady who knew the joy of serving others.

An attitude of service for the teen can be seen in small gestures such as helping a friend with a school project, or helping their grandparents replace a light bulb, or volunteering to help their youth group at church or school do a community service project. Recently, I was encouraged when I saw a group of middle-schoolers cleaning up a vacant lot that was filled with debris. In my opinion, one of the most helpful things parents and others who work with teens can do is to get them involved in serving others. The teen who gets a taste of the satisfaction that comes from serving others will likely take this trait into adulthood.

PRAISE THEM FOR DOING GOOD

When parents observe their teen in some way serving others, verbal affirmation or a handwritten note expressing how proud you are of them helps them internalize the value of serving others. One college freshman said, "My parents were always helping others. My dad took me with him often to help Habitat for Humanity build houses for the poor. I guess that is why I enjoy helping others. Last weekend I took a group of my freshman friends with me to help build a Habitat house. For some of them it was the first time they had ever done anything like that. One friend said, 'This is a whole lot more fun than playing Frisbee.' In the middle of the week, I got a card from my dad telling me how proud he was of me." Parents who affirm "service to others" as well as academic achievement are teaching their teen how to make a positive difference in the world. I wish more college students could experience this joy, rather than seeking happiness in selfish pursuits.

Parents who are upset because their teen is not consistently doing their household chores may miss opportunities for affirmation. One son was given the chore of taking out the trash daily. He missed one day, and when he did take it out his mom said, "About time you took the trash out. I was getting sick of the smell." Condemnation seldom motivates a teen, or an adult. Why not say, "I really appreciate your taking the trash out. It means a lot to me. When you take it out every evening, I don't have to smell trash the next morning. Thanks!" Affirmation given without demanding perfection motivates the teen to be consistent. When service on any level is commended, it tends to become more permanent.

I believe that every teen should have household responsibilities. These should be recognized as ways of serving the family, not simply as a job to be performed. When parents thank each other and express appreciation to the teen when a task is completed, it communicates that serving the family is a noble pursuit. An attitude of service learned in the family will later be exported to the community.

When teens observe their parents doing acts of kindness for others, the seeds are planted and will likely bear fruit in the life of the teenager. Inviting your teen to help you in serving others builds memories that will likely lead them to develop an attitude of service. Through the years, I have observed numerous parents who take a week of vacation each summer to work in their church's youth camp. Some work in the kitchen and others are counselors or athletic directors. I am not surprised that I am now seeing their adult children do the same. The influence of the parents' model cannot be overestimated. Helping our teens develop an attitude of service is equipping them for a life of deep satisfaction.

With all of our imperfections, I must say that this is one area in which I think Karolyn and I did a rather good job. Our children will never forget Karolyn's commitment to cook a hot breakfast for the family every morning until the last one left for college. For Karolyn, this was a Mother Teresa–level commitment, because she is not a morning person. We sought to exhibit an attitude of service both in the home and in the community. My vocation, as any counselor knows, requires a deep commitment to serve others. One of our great joys is to see our adult children both living a lifestyle of serving others. We also are seeing that attitude in the lives of our two grandchildren who are now in college. Yes, life's deepest satisfaction is found in serving God by serving others.

GOING DEEPER

There are plenty of books you can read about an attitude of service, but the most impactful way to form servants' hearts in your children is by inviting them to serve alongside you. Finding ways to serve with different aged children can be challenging, but below are some organizations and ideas to get you started.

GroupMissionTrips.com

Group Mission Trips offers service opportunities for entire families. Trips range from doing home repair to community service to international missions. Trips like these leave indelible marks on families.

LeaderTreks.org

Leader Treks offers youth mission trips in multiple locations throughout the United States and other countries. They can customize trips for any sized group and the Leader Treks staff takes care of all the details. You just show up and do everything from hurricane relief to putting on a neighborhood vacation Bible school.

Adventures.org—Adventures in Missions

A.I.M. offers short-term mission trips for high school and college students. They also offer nine-month mission trips they call "The World Race." These trips serve as a gap-year program after high school for seventeen to twenty year-olds.

Habitat.org—Habitat for Humanity

Habitat for Humanity is a nonprofit organization that helps families build homes. They have volunteer opportunities for all ages and even have campus chapters in many high schools.

Crazy Love: Overwhelmed by a Relentless God —by Francis Chan

Francis Chan is another person who lives out the mission he preaches. His book *Crazy Love* often resonates with teenagers and will cast a vision for your child to live a life of service and faith. You can also watch videos from the book at CrazyLoveBook.com.

Improving Your Serve: The Art of Unselfish Living
—by Charles R. Swindoll

This classic is difficult to read because it reveals much of the selfish nature that has a stronghold on our hearts. Swindoll demonstrates the true power and influence of a servant and the rich rewards that come from laying your life down for others.

THINK ABOUT IT

1. Did you observe an attitude of service in your parents? If so, how was it expressed in the family and in the community?

2. In reflecting on your own teen years, what indicates that you were beginning to develop an attitude of service?

3. As an adult, how would you rank yourself on a scale of 0–10 in having an attitude of service?

4. Do you view your vocation as a means of serving others? If so, how does this impact the manner in which you do your job?

5. What are you presently doing to help your teen develop an attitude of service?

6. Have you observed your teen serving other family members? Or serving outside the family? If so, how did you respond? Did your response have a positive or negative impact on your teen?

7. What would you like to do differently after reading this chapter?

Chapter 10

I Wish I'd Known . . .

That a Teen's Emotional Health Greatly Impacts Educational Success

I knew the value of education before we had teenagers. What I did not realize was the connection between emotional health and the academic success of the teenager. This reality was made abundantly clear as I counseled with numerous parents who were concerned about their teen's educational struggles. "We know he is smart, but he doesn't seem to be motivated." "We can't get him to take his homework seriously." "We want her to do her best, but she seems satisfied with just getting by." "Our teen keeps getting in trouble at school. It's like he just can't get along with people, including teachers." These are the kinds of statements I heard from parents.

Numerous research projects clearly reveal that students who do well in high school will be more successful in life than those who do poorly or those who drop out of high school. They are more likely to be accepted into college and do well. Educational success leads to better jobs, higher salaries, more opportunities in life, and better physical health, among other advantages. As a society, we know that quality education reduces crime and poverty as well as enhancing economic stability, social equality, and a greater sense of civic involvement. Most parents want their teens to make the most of their educational opportunities. However, many teens do not reach their potential academically.

When we think of teens who do not do well in school, we often attribute it to things like drug and alcohol abuse, gang involvement, or mental health problems. What I discovered is that often the problem is rooted in unmet emotional needs. In our highly fractured society, many teens have experienced the divorce of their parents. Others live with single moms and have never known their father. Still others have verbally or physically abusive parents, which sometimes leads to the teen being passed from foster home to foster home. It is not hard to understand why many of these teens have felt emotionally abandoned. But what about the teens who grow up in fairly stable homes, yet seem to struggle academically? I do not want to minimize problems such as Attention Deficit Hyperactivity Disorder (ADHD), dyslexia, dyscalculia, and other learning disabilities. These difficulties are being addressed by our better schools. What I want to focus on are the emotional reasons why many students do not perform well in school. When the teen's basic emotional needs are unmet, it will greatly affect their ability and motivation to pursue educational goals. What are these emotional needs, and how can parents and other caring adults help meet these needs?

In chapter 3 we discussed what I believe is the teen's most fundamental emotional need—the need to feel loved. That is why I devoted an entire chapter to that topic. Discovering and regularly speaking the teen's primary love language helps the parent effectively meet this deep emotional need. In this chapter, I want to focus on some of the other basic emotional needs of the teenager.

THE NEED TO BELONG

The need to belong is huge with teenagers. This is the emotional need that pushes teens to form cliques, join clubs, and sometimes get pulled into destructive gangs. Teens want to feel accepted— to be liked by others. A teen can be devastated by cyberbullying coming from schoolmates. When people whom they see as "friends" fail to respond to their online posts, the teen feels rejected. The most natural place for meeting the need to belong is the family. This is the heart of what family is all about. Everyone belongs. Everyone is important. Everyone is accepted. These attitudes are the marks of a healthy family.

However, when the family is fractured by divorce or absentee or abusive parents, the sense of belonging evaporates. One teen said, "My dad said he loved me, but he left us and I haven't seen him in two years." This teen was talking to a school counselor because he was doing poorly in his classes. His emotional world had been rocked and he felt rejected by his father. If I could say one thing to couples who divorce, it would be, "Please stay connected to your teenager. He/she desperately needs to feel that they are still important to you, that you genuinely care about them. If you were verbally or physically abusive to the teen before the divorce, please get counseling and deal with your own problems and apologize to the teen for your destructive behavior, and seek to rebuild a loving relationship."

What can parents do to build a family environment where teens feel they are wanted and that they belong? Obviously, one way is to regularly speak their primary love language, as we noted above. Teens who feel loved by parents are far more likely to experience a sense of belonging. Also, parents can verbally emphasize "our" sense of belonging. Talk openly about your commitment to each other. At a family conference or around the dinner table, ask: "Does everyone know that we are here for each other? We may not always agree on everything, but we are a family, and families stick together. Does everyone agree?" Let the children respond with comments or questions. Openly discussing the concept of belonging to a family and what that means helps teens feel safe and valued. Of course, our words and actions must demonstrate what we say about being a family.

The social skills of asking questions and listening, which we discussed in chapter 5, are important in demonstrating the worth of the teenager. When we ask their opinion and give them our undivided attention as they talk, we demonstrate that we value their thoughts and ideas. This enhances their sense of belonging. They feel like a valued member of the family. Conversely, when we don't involve them in conversation, they get the idea that their ideas are not important to us. This does not mean that we must always agree with their ideas. We are the parents and are ultimately responsible for making decisions we feel are best, but including the teen in the process communicates that you see their role in the family as important.

Doing things together as a family also builds the emotional bond of the family. Depending on the interests of the teen, baking and decorating cakes, working on a home repair project together, exploring local museums, historic houses, or nature preserves, attending plays and concerts or sporting events are all ways of building the sense of unity. It is memories of such experiences that will give the teen a sense of belonging that will follow them into adulthood. The sense of family belonging and being accepted will not only tend to keep the teen from turning to unhealthy gang involvement, but will also encourage them to make the most of their lives by taking school seriously.

THE NEED FOR SELF-CONFIDENCE

Teens who do not feel good about themselves and their abilities will likely not give themselves to academic pursuits. Self-confidence does not mean thinking or feeling that you are better than others. It is, rather, feeling good about who *you* are. Self-confidence gives the teen the courage to try new things, to sign up for courses about which they may know little, but want to know more. They are not trying to be like others in order to feel good about themselves. Rather, they are trying to develop the interests and abilities they have in order to reach goals that they consider worthwhile.

Self-confidence is greatly impacted by the messages the teen hears others say about him/her. I remember a young man who did poorly in high school but excelled in college. I wondered, "Why the sudden change?" In our conversation, he revealed that he had had a middle-school teacher who said to him, after he had done poorly on an exam, "I guess you are just not a student like your sister."

Those words had a devastating impact. "I stopped trying," he told me. "Why waste my time studying if I am not a good student? I liked basketball, so I gave myself to basketball." (He was an excellent player in high school.)

"But why did all this change when you got to college?" I asked.

"I took a course in philosophy and loved it. I started studying and made an A in the course. I thought, 'Maybe I am a student,' so I started studying. After that, I made good grades for the rest of my college career."

One statement from a thoughtless teacher framed his thinking about himself as a student. One positive educational experience reversed his view of himself.

Words of encouragement are extremely important in helping develop the teen's self-confidence. Parents and other significant adults sometimes fail to understand the power of words. Condemning words tend to communicate feelings of incompetence. Affirming words stimulate feelings of self-confidence. Many successful adults will say, "My parents told me I could do whatever I wanted to do in life if I would just apply myself." That message motivated them to apply themselves academically as well as in other areas of interest. The self-confident teen will likely do well in school as well as in other pursuits.

A parent's investment of time and energy in helping teens be successful in projects or goals they may pursue is another way of building self-confidence. A teen who has interest in learning to cook or bake will develop self-confidence from the parent who takes time to teach them. The same is true for parental help in sports, music, woodworking, tech, painting, or any other interest the teen may have. The more you help them be successful in their endeavors, the greater will be their sense of self-confidence. The sense of accomplishment feeds positive self-esteem, which serves the teen well in the educational setting.

THE NEED TO BE UNDERSTOOD

The current culture of our world is extremely confusing. A thousand voices communicate a thousand different views on almost everything. The teen is trying to make sense of all of this and decide what they should believe and do with their lives. In this process they will often entertain ideas that are different from the parents' beliefs on any number of topics. The wise parent will hear them out without condemning them for having such thoughts. Rather, the parent listens attentively, asking questions with a view to understanding the teen's thoughts and feelings. Condemning the teen's ideas outright without discussion pushes the teen away and leaves them feeling misunderstood. Taking time to listen keeps the door open for further dialogue.

As adults, we too want to be understood. That is why we share ideas with friends and family. We are social creatures and it is by dialogue that we build relationships. In a culture in which we are often not listening to each other but rather condemning those with whom we disagree and speaking of them in disparaging terms, a teen finds few models of dialogue on social media and elsewhere. This makes the role of the parent even more important in modeling empathetic listening. One college freshman said, "My parents have always heard me out, even when I had wild ideas. I have always felt understood by them and never condemned. They always challenged me to seek to keep learning and be open to changing ideas when I discover new information. That is one reason why education is so important to me. I want to keep learning." If parents keep the door of communication open, they will have a positive influence in the teen's life well into the college years and beyond. When the teen feels understood by parents, they are far more open to hear the parents' perspective.

This does not mean that we agree with all of their ideas. It does mean that we respect them and are always open to hearing their thoughts and feelings. We certainly share our views on the topic and why we hold them. We may share books or research that support our ideas. The ideal is that together we can continue to learn. The teen who feels understood and respected by parents will typically share their educational experience with parents. One recent college graduate said: "Because my parents included me in conversations about my education in middle school and high school, I was able to talk with them freely when it came time to choose a college. They wanted me to make the final choice, and I appreciated that, but I also wanted the value of their insights." This is the attitude we hope will emerge as we seek to meet the teen's need for being understood.

THE NEED FOR MEANING AND PURPOSE

Let's be honest: many adults still struggle with this. Just beneath the surface of daily activities is that lingering question "Am I making a difference?" In our culture, we have sought to shift this longing to such questions as: "Am I having fun? Am I happy? Do I enjoy what I am doing with my life? Am I good at what I do?" If we can respond positively to these questions, we find enough satisfaction to continue on our chosen path. If not, we tend to drift into anxiety, depression, feelings of boredom, and apathy.

For the teenager who grows up in our culture, this need for meaning and purpose is tied to the sense of accomplishment. The teen is simply following the cultural norm. People are rewarded in our culture for accomplishments. If they excel in athletics, they are applauded. They may even get a free ride to college, which is not always associated with a good education. This focus on accomplishment is what pulls many teens into video games. At first, they compete against themselves, trying to improve their skills. Then, they compete with others, enjoying each victory and feeling badly about each defeat. Achievement in the world of video games is not likely to get them a free ride to college. In fact, it is likely to hamper their academic journey.

Don't misunderstand me; I am not against accomplishment. A sense of accomplishment feeds the deep emotional need for meaning and purpose. As parents, we want to encourage this drive for accomplishment. However, we hope that we can steer that drive toward meaningful accomplishments that will be helpful to the teen and to the culture. We know that some teens get pulled into gangs and work their way through the ranks to become really accomplished at selling drugs as young adults. They have a sense of "achievement," but one that ultimately does not help them or society.

The earlier parents can help children pursue worthy goals, the more likely the teen's accomplishments will be wholesome. If we believe that educational accomplishments will thrust the teen toward a productive future, then we want to do all we can to whet the teen's appetite for education. Ideally, this journey starts with the parent reading books to the child before they are old enough to read. As the child gets older, the parent establishes "reading times" in the child's daily schedule. Thus, reading becomes an integral part of the child's life. Educators agree that reading is the most fundamental skill in obtaining a good education. Some parents have failed to build this interest and skill into the mind of the child, choosing to let the child stare at screens for endless hours. Again, educators know that a completely "screen-driven child" will not likely reach their potential in the educational world.

What if, as a parent, you realize that your teen does not have an interest in reading, but spends an inordinate amount of time daily on the screen? I suggest that you talk with a teacher who can recommend good books for a teen the age of your child. Then, let the teen know that you realize that you have failed them by not exposing them to good books. Apologize to them, and ask them to forgive you. Then work with them and their schedules to help them explore the world of non-required reading. Remember, many of today's teens are highly scheduled, and you don't want this to become another chore. Let them see *you* reading a book in your free time instead of scrolling or binge-watching. Take them to a good independent bookstore sometime—and don't forget your local public library.

We know that teens will have different areas of interest, often very passionate. If they are musically inclined, get them biographies of great musicians. If they are sports-minded, give them biographies of successful athletes. If they are interested in medicine, let them read the life stories of those who have walked that journey. Introduce them to books and authors that reflect and explore your family's ethnic heritage. If they are more inclined to science fiction and fantasy, help them discover the best of that world.

The need for meaning and purpose is far deeper than simply accomplishing personal goals. But for the teen, this is a good place to begin. In the next chapter we will address the spiritual dimension of life, which also speaks to the need for meaning and purpose.

To the degree that the emotional needs we have discussed in

this chapter are met, to that degree we are preparing our teen for educational success. Through the years, I have been surprised at how many parents have failed to see the relationship between meeting emotional needs and educational success. I hope that this chapter will help many parents make that connection.

GOING DEEPER

It's important to teach children to be unselfish. It's also necessary to train them in healthy practices of self-care. As they become more aware of their own emotions, they in turn will be able to better care for others. The resources below will help you train your teens to be compassionate, empathetic, brave, resilient, and emotionally intelligent.

Are My Kids on Track?: The 12 Emotional, Social, and Spiritual Milestones Your Child Needs to Reach
—by David Thomas, Sissy Goff, and Melissa Trevathan

At what age should my children be able to manage their emotions? That's the question this book answers. It gives parents realistic expectations on when they can expect children to hit specific emotional milestones such as learning to empathize and making faith their own.

Emotionally Healthy Spirituality: It's Impossible to Be Spiritually Mature While Remaining Emotionally Immature
—by Peter Scazzero

St. Teresa of Avila wrote, "Almost all problems in the spiritual life stem from a lack of self-knowledge." This book from one of the leading experts in emotional intelligence is, essentially, one long counseling session that allows you to understand who you are and why you are that way. If parents approach their own stories with courage, it could lead to deep vulnerability and transform their relationships with their teenagers.

Ask Alice podcast—by Rooted Ministry

Alice Churnock offers a helpful podcast for parents that addresses relevant topics like Seasonal Affective Disorder, eating disorders, depression, anxiety, suicide, birth order, sibling dynamics, and gender dysphoria. She also coaches parents in how to talk with teenagers about significant current events and hot-button issues.

The Search for Significance: Student Edition—by Robert S. McGee

Teenagers are tempted to base their self-worth on two things: their accomplishments and the opinions of others. McGee's classic helps students discover their identity in God's love for them.

"Competence, Autonomy, and Connection: Why We Play Video Games"—by Reece Akhtar*

Research shows that teenage gamers spend more than twenty hours per week playing video games. What makes them so addictive? This article explains how scientific research has revealed three psychological motivations of gamers: (1) the need to feel competent; (2) the need to possess autonomy; and (3) the need to build engaging relationships with other players. If you want to help your teens grow in emotional maturity, ask them questions related to these three categories. Their answers will help you both understand how these factors motivate them.

*You can access this article online via https://medium.com/ @ReeceAkhtar/competence-autonomy-and-connection-why-we-play-video-games-66390a6258d4.

THINK ABOUT IT

1. Reflect on your own teen years. On a scale of 0–10, rate how well the following emotional needs were met in your life.

   - The need to feel loved
   - The need to belong
   - The need for self-confidence
   - The need to be understood
   - The need for meaning and purpose

2. As you look back, what do you wish your parents had done differently? What do you appreciate about your parents?

3. Reflect on your teenager. On a scale of 0–10, rate how well you think each of these needs is being met.

4. Would you be willing to ask your teen to rate himself/herself on how well these emotional needs are being met in their life?

5. If either of you thinks there is room for improvement in any of these areas, read again the suggestions made in meeting each of these emotional needs and decide which of them might be most helpful.

6. Do you think your teen is on track to be successful in obtaining a meaningful education? What further steps might you take to enhance this possibility?

Chapter 11

I Wish I'd Known . . .

That Teens Need Spiritual Direction

All people are spiritual in some way. In my educational journey, I completed both an undergraduate and graduate degree in anthropology—the study of world cultures. Without exception, human cultures believe in a spirit world. The nature of these beliefs varies from culture to culture, but the fact that they exist reveals the spiritual nature of humanity. As a Christian, I believe this is because we are made in the image of God. We have the capacity to think, to reason, to make decisions, to be creative, and to have a relationship with the God who created us. I believe that God revealed Himself supremely through Jesus Christ; His life, death, and resurrection are the heart of the Christian message.

If we are followers of Christ, we are highly motivated to help our teens know the peace, joy, and purpose we have found in following Christ. I really believe those who have found the greatest satisfaction in life are those who have opened their lives to God, accepted His gift of forgiveness, and His power to enable them to live fruitful lives in service to others.

There are many religions in the world, but they could not all be true, for one simple reason: their beliefs often contradict each other. In our culture, teens will be exposed to many different religious traditions. They need the guidance of parents, helping them filter through the many voices that call for their devotion. Parents who take a "hands-off" approach and do not discuss religious beliefs leave their teen to the influence of peers or other adults who will seek to influence them. Some teens end up in cultic groups that distort reality and lead to a lifestyle that is detrimental to the teen's well-being.

"WHAT IF I'M NOT RELIGIOUS?"

For parents who are not satisfied with their own spiritual journey, this may seem like a daunting task. One parent asked, "How can I help my teen when I am not a religious person myself?" Another parent said, "I'm not sure I want my teen to end up where I am. I need help myself on understanding the God thing." All of us have been influenced by someone when it comes to our view of spirituality. As adults, we are not too old to examine or reexamine our own journey and explore the possibility of finding what some have called "soul rest" in knowing God.

Most of the world's religions have one commonality. They have developed a system of what one must do in order to be accepted by God or to gain a higher level of spiritual understanding. Christianity

is very different. The Christian believes that God initiates a relationship with us rather than our seeking to find an unknown god.
God, the Creator, reached out to us in the person of Jesus Christ,
His Son. He was more than a mere man, for no man could do the
things He did. Though He was put to death by Roman soldiers, He
said about His life, "No one takes it from me, but I lay it down of my
own accord."[1] Those who murdered Him thought they were ending
His life, but in reality, three days after being placed in the grave, He
arose from the dead and appeared for over forty days to over five
hundred people. To all who believe in Him, He promised that they
too would live beyond the grave with Him.

Yes, the teachings of Jesus clearly show us how best to invest our
lives and we seek to follow His teachings, but not in order to be accepted by God. It is because we have been accepted by Him, and our
deep desire is to please Him. We know that when we are following
His teachings, we will accomplish the greatest good with our lives.
Thus, we are highly motivated to invest time in helping our teens
understand what it means to be a true follower of Jesus.

In this chapter, I want to suggest practical ways to engage our
teens in conversation about our own religious beliefs, while helping
them explore the beliefs of others. Ultimately, teenagers must decide
what they will believe and how they will live their lives. What they
believe about God will definitely impact every aspect of their lives.
I believe that parents can play a significant role in guiding the teen
to wise decisions.

The process begins with parents exploring the foundation of
their own beliefs. Most of us came to adulthood with some religious
beliefs, which we learned from parents or other significant people
in our childhood or youth. So, we identify ourselves as Buddhist,

Muslim, Christian, atheist, and so on because that is the culture in which we grew up. Many times we have never explored the history associated with our religious beliefs. When we become parents, we are asking, "Do I want my children to believe what I believe about God?" If we are not certain, then it is time to explore the foundation on which our beliefs rest.

"PART OF OUR CONVERSATION"

I did this when I was in college, and came down affirmed in my Christian faith, not simply as a belief system but also as a personal relationship with God. I have never regretted that decision. It is God's work in my life that gave me the motivation to love and serve my wife, to love and serve my children, and to serve others. Therefore, I wanted my children to come to know and experience God's love and accomplish God's purposes for their lives.

So, in the early years, we read Bible stories to both our daughter and her younger brother. We prayed for and with them every night as we put them to bed. When they became teenagers, God talk was not a new thing in our family. We read Scriptures together and discussed their meaning. We encouraged them to ask questions and share their ideas. Talking about God and the Bible was a part of our conversation just as we talked about sports, music, and other subjects.

We wanted them to have the benefit of hearing others teach the Bible and discuss its application to life. So, we took them to church and encouraged them to be a part of all the activities provided by the church for teens. We tried to create an environment in which they felt free to ask questions about God, the Bible, and what it meant to be a Christian. They both became followers of Christ. Now, as adults, they are both deeply committed to investing their lives in serving others. John, the Christian apostle, once said, "I have no greater joy than to hear that my children are walking in the truth."[2] Karolyn and I know that joy! As parents, we must not force our beliefs on our teens, but we certainly want to expose them to the God who has guided our lives.

In a multicultural society, your teen will likely be exposed to friends who grew up in various religious traditions (or no tradition). I strongly encourage parents to teach their teens to respect the beliefs of others. I also suggest that parents expose their teens to the basic beliefs of other religions so they can talk intelligently with their friends of a different faith. One resource is *Christ Among Other gods* by Erwin Lutzer.[3] Teens also need to read books that explain why Christians believe what they believe. I recommend two books written by Lee Strobel, a former atheist who became a Christian after carefully examining the evidence. The titles are *The Case for Christ*[4] and *The Case for Faith*.[5]

Since Christianity is not a set of rules but a relationship with God, I would hope that parents would teach the teen how to have a daily conversation with God. The Bible is often called "the Word of God." Thus, God speaks to us through "His Word." So a conversation with God involves reading a chapter in the Bible each day and talking to God about what we read. We might thank Him for the truth of what we have read, confess our failures and ask forgiveness, request His power to do what He has said, or say, "I don't understand what that means." It is simply having an honest conversation with God. The teen who builds this into their daily schedule is likely to have a growing relationship with God.

If the parents are also having a daily conversation with God, they may sometimes share with the teen what they read and their response. The teen will likely reciprocate on some days. They may also ask the parent about something they read but did not understand. This leads to meaningful conversation about spiritual things. They need not be daily conversations, but they will likely be meaningful conversations.

WHAT JESUS REALLY SAID

You might consider challenging your teen to read the book of John in the New Testament. It was written by one of the twelve disciples, and John shares much of what Jesus said and did. Perhaps ask your teen to make a list of all the things Jesus taught us to do and another list of all the things He taught us not to do. The teachings of Jesus were given because He loves us and wants us to have a great life. The teen will also get a clear picture of what Jesus said about Himself and His purpose in coming to earth. If the two of you read one chapter in the book of John each day for the next three weeks and discussed what you were learning, you might have some really good discussions.

Another practice that enhances our relationship with God is memorizing key verses of the Bible. What if the parent and teen agreed to memorize one verse each month? Select verses that have implications for daily life. Print the verses on cards so they are easy to access. Several times a day, read them aloud, until they begin to settle in your mind. From time to time, quote them to each other. The prophet Jeremiah said this to God: "Your words are what sustain me. They bring me great joy and are my heart's delight, for I bear your name."[6] That may also become our response as we memorize God's Word.

PRAYING FOR YOUR TEEN

As you read the Bible and see something that you would like to see in the life of your teen, ask God to make that a reality for them. Pray that God will give them wisdom in their decisions. Pray that He will bring into their lives people who will enrich their lives and keep them from people who would lead them into a destructive life-style. Pray also that God will give you wisdom in how best to relate to your teen. Someone has said, "God gave us teenagers to keep us on our knees."

God intends parents to play a key role in helping teens come to understand and respond to God's love for them. To ancient Israel God said: "Teach [these commands] to your children, talking about them when you sit at home and when you walk along the road, when you lie down and when you get up."[7] If you aren't sure how to talk about such things, ask God for wisdom. He will help you. If God is very much a living part of your life, make sure you're modeling that to your teen. (See next chapter for more.)

I hope that some of these ideas will help you in your role of giving spiritual guidance to your teen. If you are in the process of re-thinking your own spiritual beliefs, I would encourage you to reach out to a local pastor or someone you believe could help. A relationship with God is similar to human relationships in that it is a daily process of growing closer to each other. Jesus said, "Come unto me, all you who are weary and burdened, and I will give you rest. Take my yoke upon you and learn from me, for I am gentle and humble in heart, and you will find rest for your souls."[8] That invitation is still open to anyone who will come to Him.

GOING DEEPER

When you think back on your teenage years, what do you wish would have been different? Did you have an older mentor to help guide you in the faith? If not, how could that have impacted the direction of your life? Studies show that one key factor in a teenager's faith development is having a healthy relationship with an adult who is not their parent. If you want to provide spiritual direction for your child, consider finding a tag-team partner who doesn't live in your house— maybe a coach, a teacher, an uncle, a grandmother, or a youth leader.

While it may work for you to use the resources below with your child, you may also consider sharing these ideas with someone who can partner with you in mentoring your teen.

BibleProject.com

BibleProject is an animation studio that produces free Bible videos, podcasts, blogs, classes, and educational resources to help make the biblical story more accessible. If you want your kids to better understand God's Word, BibleProject YouTube videos are a great place to begin.

RightNowMedia.org

RightNow Media is the world's largest library of biblical video resources. They offer some free content and some paid subscriptions through your local church or nonprofit. It's the "Netflix" of Christian discipleship videos.

AlphaUSA.org

Alpha is a video discipleship series of sessions exploring the Christian faith. There are both student and adult versions of these courses. These videos are ideal for people who are newer to the faith. Each of the eleven talks looks at a different question around faith and facilitates conversation. Alpha courses are run all around the globe and open to anyone.

EmilyPFreeman.com

Emily offers a blog and podcast called *The Next Right Thing*. It's a podcast focused on spiritual direction and helping you make wise decisions. Sometimes listening to a podcast during a car ride with your teenager feels more manageable than having a self-led conversation. A parent of teenagers herself, Emily asks questions that can spark meaningful discussion between you and your children.

The Blue Book: A Devotional Guide for Every Season of Your Life—by Jim Branch

This devotional is teen-appropriate, a yearlong guide including scripture, ancient prayers, and daily reflections.

Sticky Faith: Everyday Ideas to Build Lasting Faith in Your Kids —by Dr. Kara E. Powell and Dr. Chap Clark

This easy-to-read discipleship tool offers parents a powerful strategy for encouraging their children's spiritual growth so that it will stick with them into adulthood. It coaches parents in having difficult conversations around such topics as "not wanting to go to church."

Scripture Memorization

Dr. Chapman recommends twelve brief passages from the Bible for parents and teens to memorize. They are Psalm 119:9–11; Isaiah

41:10; John 3:16; Romans 6:23; 1 Corinthians 10:13; Philippians 4:6–7; Galatians 5:22; John 13:34–35; John 14:6; Matthew 11:28–29; 1 Timothy 4:12; and Philippians 2:4. Read them in a more contemporary version like the New Living Translation or the New International Version. If you don't have a Bible around the house, go to YouVersion.com and download their app.

THINK ABOUT IT

1. How equipped do you feel to give spiritual guidance to your teen? What could you do to feel more comfortable with this?

2. When your teen was a child, did you seek to share with them your beliefs about God? As you look back, are there things you wish you had done differently?

3. Are you at a place where you recognize that your teen needs spiritual guidance? If so, what are you doing to help them process their own thoughts about God?

4. Would you be open to challenging them to try having a daily conversation with God as described in this chapter? Would you be willing to do this yourself?

5. Are you involved in a church and is your teen also involved? If not, would you be open to exploring that possibility? Whom could you ask to help you find a church that might be a positive influence on your teen?

6. What suggestion in this chapter would you like to implement with your teen? What steps do you need to take to get started?

I Wish I'd Known . . .

That a Parent's Model Is More Important Than Their Words

Throughout this book, I have focused on realities that parents need to know about their teen's emotional, intellectual, social, and spiritual needs. My goal has been to share with parents what I wish I had known before our children became teenagers. If you have read to this point, you know that I have given practical ideas on how to effectively meet these needs. In most chapters I have alluded to the importance of the parents' model. In this chapter

I want to focus on the power of our example.

Before we had teenagers, I was fully aware of my parental responsibility to teach and train them in the many areas we have discussed in the book. What I did not realize is that the way I lived my life would have a greater impact than my words. This reality does not minimize the value of teaching and training, but it maximizes the value of my model. To the degree that I practice what I teach, to that degree the teen is likely to listen and apply what I teach. When teens observe a gap between what I teach and the way I live, they are likely to take lightly what I say. Thus, my model is more important than my words.

There is an old saying that goes something like this: "Like mother, like daughter. Like father, like son." I don't know the origin of that statement, but I have observed the truth of its message as I have counseled parents and teens. An alcoholic father often has an alcoholic son. A mother who has a controlling personality will often have a daughter who does the same. A father who abuses his wife and children will often have a son who abuses others. It is common knowledge among counselors that those who have been abused, often abuse.

This does not mean that the parental model must be repeated. No! With the proper help, a teen can learn from a negative example. That is the desired outcome of every counselor. We are not destined to repeat the poor example of our parents, but we are greatly impacted by their example. That is why the role of school counselors and other counselors is so important in the life of teens who are raised in less-than-ideal environments.

Parents who are genuinely seeking to give their teens the best chance of reaching their potential in life must seek to model what they teach. Saying to a teen, "Do as I say, not as I do," may make you feel "in charge," but it will not develop character in your teen. What you do speaks so loudly, they cannot hear what you say. However, when your actions reflect the things you teach, then your words enhance the teen's understanding of what you are saying.

One of the most sobering questions I have ever asked myself is: "What if my teen turns out to be just like me?" I did not ask that question when they were children. I asked it when they were teens and I began to see in them some of the traits that I saw in myself; some positive and some not so positive. The soberness of that question helped me make changes in my life, some of which I have shared in this book.

I invite you to be brave and ask yourself the following questions. What if my teen grows up to:

Handle anger the way I handle anger?

Treat their spouse the way I treat my spouse?

Drive a car the way I drive a car?

Have the same work ethic that I have?

Talk to other people the way I talk to others?

Talk about people who are "different" from them in the same way that I do?

Respond to alcohol or drugs the way I do?

Have the same quality of relationship with God that I have?

Handle their money the way I handle my money?

Treat their in-laws the way I treat mine?

Treat their teenagers the way I am treating them?

Apologize when they are unkind in the same way that I apologize?

Forgive those who apologize to them in the way that I forgive others?

You may want to add a few questions of your own.

Okay, so this is a really somber challenge, but I give it because I hope you will ask these kinds of questions much earlier than I did. You need not wait until you see your teen mimicking your behavior. With a little reflection, you can identify the things that need to be changed in the way you have been living your life. We teach our teens to be kind, courteous, patient, forgiving, humble, generous, and honest. So let's work at demonstrating those qualities in our own lives.

When I was a teen, my parents taught me many wholesome principles to live by. Here are a few of those principles:

Always do what you say you will do.

Recognize every individual as important and treat them with respect.

Remember that life is not about fame or money. It is about using your abilities to help others.

Treat others the way you would like to be treated.

Put God first and seek to follow the teachings of Jesus.

Always tell the truth.

Never forget that every decision you make has consequences.

Always apologize when you do wrong or hurt someone.

Why do I remember these principles as an adult? Not because my parents often repeated these words, but because I saw these lived out in their lives. In this book, I have shared eleven things I wish I'd known before we had teenagers. Most of them are things we teach and train our teens. That is, we use words and actions in an effort to help them learn the skills, attitudes, and behaviors that are necessary to leading a successful life. What I am emphasizing in this last chapter is the importance of the way we model these teachings in our own lives.

Those of us who have acknowledged our own failures to God and accepted His forgiveness have the help of God in making needed changes. Many of us can identify with Paul, an apostle in the early church, who said: "So I find this law at work: Although I want to do good, evil is right there with me."[1] Self-effort is not enough. But later Paul said, "I can do all this through him who gives me strength."[2] God takes pleasure in helping His children make needed changes. The good news is, we can be the kind of person that if our teen turned out to be like us, we would be pleased. That has been my goal since I had my "wake-up call" several years ago. That is also my desire for you.

GOING DEEPER

Your life speaks louder than your words. If you want your kids to become readers, they need to catch glimpses of you reading books, not just your text messages or the news. If you want your teenagers to have healthy friendships, first consider how they might describe the friendships you have modeled for them. What does your relationship as an adult look like with your aging parents? What does that model for your kids?

These questions can feel convicting, but they are simply invitations to confess to your children specific areas where you would personally like to grow. Below are some resources to help you live a life that you would want your kids to emulate.

OTHER MARRIAGE BOOKS BY DR. GARY CHAPMAN

- *The Marriage You've Always Wanted*
- *Loving Your Spouse When You Feel Like Walking Away*
- *Things I Wish I'd Known Before We Got Married*
- *Building Love Together in Blended Families* (with Ron R. Deal)
- Additionally, *The 5 Love Languages* is indispensable for couples or anyone wanting to enhance their relationships.

PARENTING RESOURCES

WonderDads.com

This is a paid subscription site that helps busy dads connect with their kids by offering personalized email recommendations of activities based on the ages of your children.

Praying the Scriptures for Your Teens: Opening the Door for God's Provision in Their Lives—by Jodie Berndt

This book is a guide to help you in praying about everything from your teen's character and safety to the purposes and plans that God has for his or her future.

ImaginativePrayer.com—by Jared Patrick Boyd

This website and book of the same name offer resources to help parents notice and nurture the work of God in their child's life. While designed for younger children, the prayer exercises are theologically rich and could be life-giving to kids and adults of all ages. Imaginative Prayer is a unique and creative way to help your children engage with their imaginations and with God Himself.

PrimalPath.com

The Primal Path is a paid video course from New York–based pastor Jon Tyson to help overwhelmed, but determined, fathers create an intentional process for walking their sons from adolescence into manhood.

The God-Centered Mom Podcast—with Heather McFadden

This down-to-earth mother of four boys shares her struggles with humor and vulnerability. If you need to laugh and to be encouraged, check out this podcast.

SPIRITUAL LEADERSHIP

Strengthening the Soul of Your Leadership: Seeking God in the Crucible of Ministry—by Ruth Haley Barton

It is easy to get so caught up in parenting that it seemingly overtakes your life and soul. In this book, Ruth Haley Barton invites her readers to an honest exploration of what happens when those in leadership roles lose track of their souls. If you want to lead your children well, you must first strengthen your own soul.

The Seven Checkpoints for Student Leaders: Seven Principles Every Teenager Needs to Know—by Andy Stanley and Stuart Hall

Initially created for youth leaders, this book lays out a blueprint that is also helpful for parents. Stanley and Hall identify seven "checkpoints" they believe are the most critical issues facing teens: (1) Authentic Faith; (2) Spiritual Disciplines; (3) Moral Boundaries; (4) Healthy Friendships; (5) Wise Choices; (6) Ultimate Authority; and (7) Others First.

THINK ABOUT IT

1. What are some of the principles that your parents taught you when you were a teenager? How well did they demonstrate these principles in their own lives?

2. As you consider how well you model what you want your teen to learn, would you be willing to ask the somber questions that we posed in this chapter? What if my teen grows up to:

Handle anger the way I handle anger?

Treat their spouse the way I treat my spouse?

Drive a car the way I drive a car?

Have the same work ethic that I have?

Talk to other people the way I talk to others?

Talk about other people who are different the way I talk about them?

Handle conflicts the way I handle conflicts?

Treat their in-laws the way I treat mine?

Treat their teenagers the way I am treating mine?

Apologize when they are unkind in the same way that I apologize?

Forgive those who apologize to them in the way I forgive others?

Handle their money the way I do mine?

Respond to drugs or alcohol the way I do?

Have the same quality of relationship with God that I do?

In which of these areas would you like to make changes? Which one would you like to focus on first? What steps will you take this week?

3. Would you be willing to ask God to help you make these changes?

4. Consider asking your teen this question: "If you could change one thing about me that would make me a better parent, what would you like to see changed?" Their answer may help you focus on changes that would be meaningful to your teen. The very fact that you asked the question exhibits an attitude of openness to growth, which we hope will become the attitude of your teen.

Epilogue

For many years, I have invested a great deal of my life in helping couples prepare for marriage. I believe that if couples spent as much time preparing for marriage as they do preparing for the wedding, they would have better marriages. I believe that the same principle is true when it comes to parenting. If couples spent as much time preparing for parenting as they do in preparing for the delivery of the baby, they could be better parents. Most couples do not read a book on parenting or attend a class on the topic before they give birth to a child. Likewise, most parents do not read a book or attend a class on the topic of parenting teenagers before their child becomes a teen.

If you have read this book before your child has reached the teen years, you are among the minority who know that preparing for a task makes the task much easier. If you are reading this book in the midst of parenting a teenager, you are in the majority who wait for the wheel to squeak before they run for the oil. Whether you are in the majority or the minority, I hope that you have found the book to be helpful. As long as your teen is still in the house, it is never too late to improve your parenting style.

The first step is often identifying our failures and sincerely apologizing to our teen. One father said, "When I was willing to say to my teenage son, 'I have been reflecting on my life and I realize that I have failed you in many ways,' my relationship with my son took a giant step forward. In fact, when I shared my failures and asked forgiveness, my son not only forgave me, but acknowledged some of his failures. It was so emotionally liberating for both of us." This father is demonstrating the powerful healing that takes place when parents accept responsibility for their own failures. Apology and forgiveness open the door to making positive changes that lead to a healthy parent-teen relationship.

As someone once said, "The best thing about the future is that it comes one day at a time." As we make small or large changes in the way we live our lives and relate to our teen on a daily basis, we will make the most of our future. Teens are like clay, open to being molded by parents who genuinely love them. Above everything I have said in this book, nothing is more important than meeting the teen's need for love. If you have not yet discovered the primary love language of your teen, let me encourage you to do so and speak it on a regular basis. The teen who feels loved is far more open to the parent's words.

If your teen is struggling with deep emotional, mental, or behavioral problems, I would urge you to seek professional help. If they have had problems at school, the school counselor may be a place to begin. Parents often ask, "Where do I find the right counselor?" You may talk with a local pastor who will likely know the local counselors.

Parenting teens is not easy, but it can be extremely rewarding. When you see them developing their potential in the teen years and beyond, you will be drinking from the fountain of satisfaction. Karolyn and I find great joy in seeing how our adult children are investing in their marriages and how they are investing their vocational lives in helping others. And, yes, we take great joy in seeing our college-age grandchildren making the most of their educational opportunities. For this, we are extremely grateful. We would hope the same for all parents of teens.

I hope that you have found this book helpful. If so, please recommend it to your friends who are facing the challenge of parenting teenagers. For additional resources, visit www.5lovelanguages.com.

— GARY CHAPMAN

Acknowledgments

I want to thank all the parents who have sat in my office and shared their struggles related to their teenagers. Their openness and our discussions have helped me greatly in knowing the present challenge of rearing teens. I am also grateful for the teens who have shared their struggles.

As always, I am grateful for my wife, Karolyn, who is the first editor of my manuscripts. The Northfield Publishing team, as with all of my books, has been very supportive in making this book a reality. A special word of thanks to Betsey Newenhuyse for all of her editorial suggestions. John Hinkley has also been a constant encourager and advisor, which I deeply appreciate.

My own children, Shelley and Derek, who were once teenagers, helped me remember their own journey through the teen years. My grandson, Elliott, and granddaughter, Davy Grace, have also contributed to my understanding of the current world of teenagers. Again, I want to thank Drew Hill for his insightful comments and gathering of helpful resources that are shared throughout the book.

Notes

CHAPTER 9—I Wish I'd Known . . . That Teens Need to Learn an Attitude of Service

1. Matthew 20:28.
2. John 13:34.

CHAPTER 11—I Wish I'd Known . . . That Teens Need Spiritual Direction

1. John 10:18.
2. 3 John 4.
3. Erwin Lutzer, *Christ Among Other gods* (Chicago: Moody Publishers, 2016).
4. Lee Strobel, *The Case for Christ* (Grand Rapids: Zondervan, 1998).
5. Lee Strobel, *The Case for Faith* (Grand Rapids: Zondervan, 2000).
6. Jeremiah 15:16 NLT.
7. Deuteronomy 11:19.
8. Matthew 11:28–29.

CHAPTER 12—I Wish I'd Known . . . That a Parent's Model Is More Important Than Their Words

1. Romans 7:21.
2. Philippians 4:13.

MORE FROM DR. GARY CHAPMAN

Bestselling author and marriage counselor Gary Chapman believes that divorce is the lack of preparation for marriage. This practical book is packed with wisdom and tips to develop a loving, supportive, and mutually beneficial marriage. It's the type of information Gary himself wished he had before he got married. Dating or engaged couples will enjoy the "Talking It Over" sections.

978-0-8024-8183-2

Things I Wish I'd Known Before We Became Parents has one goal: prepare young and expectant parents for the joys and challenges of raising kids. With professional insight and advice from personal experience, Drs. Gary Chapman and Shannon Warden walk you through the ins and outs of rearing young children.

978-0-8024-1474-8

also available as eBook and audiobook

NORTHFIELD
PUBLISHING

STRUGGLING TO CONNECT WITH YOUR TEEN?

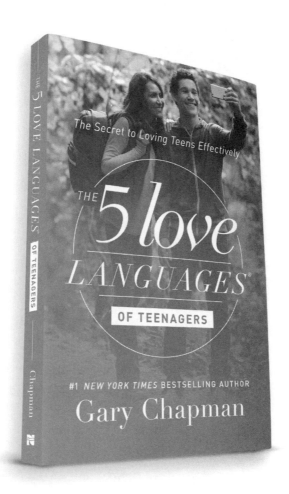

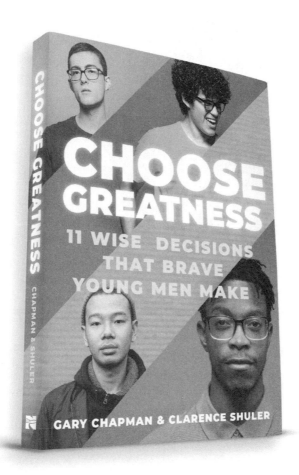